T0171657

THE WORLD
ACCORDING TO YOU!

How Our Choices Create It All

Carla L Picardi

BALBOA.PRESS

A DIVISION OF HAY HOUSE

Balboa Press books may be ordered through booksellers or by contacting:

Balboa Press
A Division of Hay House
1663 Liberty Drive
Bloomington, IN 47403
www.balboapress.com
844-682-1282

ISBN: 978-1-4525-4558-5 (sc)
ISBN: 978-1-4525-4559-2 (hc)
ISBN: 978-1-4525-4557-8 (e)

Library of Congress Control Number: 2012900690

Because of the dynamic nature of the Internet, any web addresses or
links contained in this book may have changed since publication and
may no longer be valid. The views expressed in this work are solely those
of the author and do not necessarily reflect the views of the publisher,
and the publisher hereby disclaims any responsibility for them.

The author of this book does not dispense medical advice or prescribe the use
of any technique as a form of treatment for physical, emotional, or medical
problems without the advice of a physician, either directly or indirectly. The
intent of the author is only to offer information of a general nature to help
you in your quest for emotional and spiritual well-being. In the event you use
any of the information in this book for yourself, which is your constitutional
right, the author and the publisher assume no responsibility for your actions.

Cover image by KUMOdesign

Print information available on the last page.

Balboa Press rev. date: 01/22/2024

to Leo and Madeline
my parents
thank you for your undying love,
sacrifice and support
I am much of who I am because of you

to Goffredo
amore mio
my husband, friend and soul mate
thank you for holding the full-length mirror
—through you I am learning to love unconditionally

THE HERO'S ADVENTURE

"We have not to risk the adventure alone, for the heroes of all time have gone before us. The labyrinth is thoroughly known. We have only to follow the thread of the hero path and where we had thought to find an abomination, we shall find a god. And where we had thought to slay another, we shall slay ourselves. Where we had thought to travel outward, we will come to the center of our own existence. And where we had thought to be alone, we will be with all the world."

JOSEPH CAMPBELL

CONTENTS

Foreword xi
Introduction 1

PART I: Being Positive 9

Chapter 1: Attracting Positive 11

Being Positive Creates More Positive 11
How We Create Our Lives 14
The Law of Attraction 20
The Discipline of Being Positive 27

**Chapter 2: The Role of Happiness and
Appreciation** 35

Why is Choosing Happiness Important? 35
Our Stories and Their Role in Creating Our Lives 41
Resilience and Finding the Gift 46

Chapter 3: What's Love Got to Do With It? 57

Love and Fear 57
Love, Fear and Leadership 61
We are All Things . . . We are That Too 70

PART II: Our Life is Our Illusion 81

Chapter 4: Exposing the Illusion 83

. . . and it is All an Illusion 83
How Does the Illusion Work? 86
Responsibility for Creating Our Lives 90

Chapter 5: It's All About Perspective 97

Changing our Perspective 97
Remembering How to Dream..100
Fulfillment is a State of Being 105

PART III: Our Relationships are Our Mirror................. 111

Chapter 6: Seeing Ourselves Clearly 113

Seeing Ourselves in Relation to Others 113
It's Not About Being Perfect..119
The Courage to See Our Reflection.................................123

Chapter 7: Being Who We Desire Others to Be........... 137

Finding the Love We Believe We Deserve........................137
Listening as a Way to See Our Reflection.........................143

PART IV: Our Choices Create Our World 155

Chapter 8: Are You Part of the Problem or Part of the Solution? 157

Be the Change..157
The Buck Stops Here 170

Chapter 9: The Courage to Embrace Something New... 179

Finding Balance..179
Choice → Change → Create 183

Acknowledgments 187
About the Author 191
My Book List 193

FOREWORD
by Arielle Ford

One of my favorite sayings is this:

"Being realistic is socially acceptable pessimism."

Those who continually insist that we must manage our expectations and be "realistic" (however well intentioned they may be) are simply unaware of the sheer power that we embody to create the life we want, once we have the understanding and tools to turn our desires into reality.

If I had spent my life being "realistic," today I would be living in a trailer park in Dania, Florida working as a dental hygienist. Not that there is anything wrong with that lifestyle, it's just what my parents had predicted for me. I was a lousy and uninterested student, without much of a work ethic, and no vision for my future. Fortunately I was clear that I wanted something much more and I trusted that eventually I would discover my calling. Along the way I searched for clues by studying successful people, attending human potential workshops, and reading hundreds of books. I learned how to consciously take responsibility for my thoughts, actions, and emotions and ultimately I manifested my heart's desires in every area of my life. And you can do it too!

While the majority of us were never taught these important life skills in grade school or University . . . it's not too late!

If you are ready to lead a joyful, successful, productive life then congratulations, the book you now hold in your hands is an expert guide that will show you the way.

This genuinely useful book, by my dear friend Carla Picardi, provides clear, simple, step-by-step information on how to create the life of your dreams. It's not magic, but rather age-old science combined with the latest in positive psychology and other research that allows us to become the highest and best versions of ourselves.

Carla has the best possible credentials to write a book such as this: as a highly successful architectural and design consultant, she has worked on massive, prize-winning projects that have changed the skyline of London as well as numerous other impressive projects, large and small. A respected mentor and coach she lectures around the world on a variety of topics, always guiding people with her wit and wisdom. She has spent a lifetime studying, reading and practicing these life-enhancing modalities and has a proven track record of success with them. She now reveals the best of the best, what has worked for her and so many others to create a life filled with love, laughter, prosperity, success and good health.

And, isn't that what all of us truly strive for in our lives?

Imagine waking up each day excited, enthusiastic and filled with energy to run, jump, play and create! This is what's possible when you choose to rewrite the story of your life and begin to manage your thoughts, beliefs and desires for the future.

So many of us live our lives with unresolved hurts, persistent unease and unmet goals wondering why things never quite seem to work out the way we would like them to. We were raised to believe that success only comes as a result of hard work and luck. While that can be true for some, what is more true is this:

Using the techniques and embracing the concepts shared in this book, along with dedicating yourself to the application of these great ideas, will quickly bring you satisfying results.

Whether you are 18 or 80, the pages you are about to read offer a brilliant formula for tapping into our highest potential. I predict this book will change many people's lives for the better.

Including yours.

Arielle Ford, author of *The Soulmate Secret* and *Wabi Sabi Love: The Ancient Art of Finding Perfect Love in Imperfect Relationships*

INTRODUCTION

"Things do not change; we change"

HENRY DAVID THOREAU

One of my great mentors used to say, "In your 20s you know not you know not, in your 30s you *know* you know not, in your 40s you know not you know, and in your 50s you know you know but by then it is too late!" It was my first year in London and I had just turned 30 when I realized how very little I knew about my role in the world I was creating, the waves my actions set into motion, and the damage I was leaving behind in my wake. I was not prepared for the impact of realizing that my own behavior was actually creating my discomfort. What I saw about myself was not so flattering . . . and that was only the tip of the iceberg! Fortunately, many great teachers, mentors, books and seminars found their way to me, each one providing a piece of the foundation that enabled me to create the extraordinarily rich life I have today.

If I had the book you are now holding in your hands when I was first starting out in my career, I might have understood sooner that it was always all about me . . . who I was being in every moment of my life was literally creating my life. This change of perspective might have helped me take full responsibility for my role in the creation of everything unfolding around me, and it might have prevented some unnecessary pain and drama for me and the people whose lives were interwoven with mine.

I was raised in a middle class home, went to local Catholic schools, played sports, was a high school cheerleader, and in many ways, had a typical American upbringing. I was brought up to believe that if I worked hard, did well and was respectful and tolerant of others, I would be rewarded with success. This belief system functioned well for an ambitious over-achiever in her 20s. By the time I entered my 30s, however, I realized that while "shoving a square peg into a round hole" produces results through sheer force and determination, it is extremely exhausting.

From the time I graduated from university in 1977, I worked like a crazy woman for 25 years, building the career of my dreams as an architectural designer, facilities director, project executive and property developer. I helped to create some of London's most remarkable buildings and places, which altered the skyline, changed the way large developments are managed, and enhanced London's status as a world financial center. Along the way I traveled extensively to exotic lands and socialized with all kinds of people, from street vendors to ministers of state. I studied with ancient masters, gurus, esteemed university professors and self-help authors—all the while soaking in architecture, art, design, music and culture of every kind. Funny enough, I believe my biggest achievements came from developing an understanding of my role in the events of my life and learning to make the kinds of choices that support my dreams.

One of the most profound things I came to understand, both from my life experiences and from managing teams of people working together on complex projects, is how difficult it is for most of us to see the role we play in the events of our lives. Time and time again I have seen hardworking, intelligent, creative, well-intentioned people (myself included) sabotage some area of our lives simply because most of us do not see ourselves clearly, nor do we understand that we actually have a role in creating our micro and macro world. The problem, I came to realize, rarely lies in how we go about performing the tasks of our professional and personal lives—what I call the *doing*. It is who we are *being* while we are performing those tasks and the choices that unfold from our state of *being* that really count.

The recognition that our choices create our lives is a concept most find difficult to grasp, and I understand not everyone is attracted to or ready for this level of self-inquiry. It takes fierce courage and great discipline to observe what our role has been and continues to be in the dramas that unfold around us. Usually it is not until we reach the point that we are inconsolable and desperate for things to change: a spouse walks out for no apparent reason, a life-threatening disease is diagnosed, a job is lost or a career is shattered; any number of personal crises may send us tumbling into a pit of despair. We hit rock bottom—the proverbial dark night of the soul—and are driven to uncover the answers for this overwhelmingly sad place in which we find ourselves. We may ask ourselves what we have done to deserve this tragic event, but too often in our search for answers we are blinded by shadows and illusions. Then, in an attempt to render the incident digestible, we make up stories in which someone or something else is the villain and the cause of our suffering.

Some, like me, may cling to being right (even when we are not); others lash out in blame, or become ensconced in playing the role of victim. These are all forms of self-inflicted suffering that leave us feeling frustrated and powerless. We pretend that we have no part in what is unfolding around us, and in so doing, we lose the ability to see the role we played in creating the unwanted situation in the first place. Of even greater consequence is that we give away our power to create the fulfilling lives we truly desire. There comes a moment, however, when somewhere deep within we can no longer ignore that we have a role in the chaos around us. This recognition enables us to surrender, to embrace our vulnerability, and to say—*Ok! Ok! I give up. I need help.* Once we realize that we create it all—the good, the bad and the ugly—and that we are not victims of the fickle finger of fate or an angry, punishing God, we can consciously make the choices that serve us most.

Once I actually realized my role in creating the outcomes in my life, I did not feel shame, frustration or even hopelessness; I had a genuine feeling of empowerment. Even though initially I did not see the full magnitude of how I was creating the events of my life, I finally accepted that I had a role in creating them, and this meant that I could also have a role in creating something different. I began to comprehend that the more I could let go of my need to be right and to be seen as perfect (two of my greatest challenges), the more easily and authentically I could accept myself, others, and situations—without painful and unrealistic expectations or rigid, perfectionist-driven behaviors. Over the years, I have become skilled in the art of personal happiness, peace and fulfillment. I have learned some simple yet profound concepts that help me perform at a higher level, and allow me not only to take back my power but to use it to live more fully and lead more wisely. With this I understood that if it was possible for me to have learned these skills, then it is possible for me to teach them to others as well.

The first and most important concept I learned and will share with you here is the understanding that every relationship, event, and drama in our lives reflects back to us who we are being, moment by moment. The relationships and circumstances in which we find ourselves serve as a huge full-length mirror constantly reflecting back to us who we are being. Sometimes we like what we see, especially if we have had time to adjust ourselves into the perfect pose, stand up straight, hold in the stomach, lift up the chin and smile. Most of the time however, we are living our lives on autopilot and what gets reflected back is not quite so pleasing. On the pages that follow, we will explore this concept in much greater detail, and for now, consider this: *If we do not change the image in front of the mirror, what gets reflected back will be the same image that we do not like.* We are creating it all—the peaceful beauty and the daily upheaval. It is not just happening to us as poor innocent victims, we are generating it, moment to moment, through our feelings of worthiness or unworthiness, and the thoughts, words and actions that arise as a result.

Thoughts, feelings, words and actions are energy, and each one is like tossing a boomerang very far away from ourselves. We may forget that we threw it, but that does not stop it from coming back to us. It may even hit us upside the head when we least expect it. Most of us are unaware of the energetic boomerangs we hurl into the universe on a daily basis, and are mystified when one comes back to us in a hurtful way. Yet if we are totally honest with ourselves, we will admit that we, in fact, are the ones who threw it. We still may not comprehend the degree to which we create the net result—joy or pain; satisfaction or frustration—and, once we are willing to acknowledge the part we play in the circumstances of our lives, we can begin to adjust what we are sending out in order to ensure different results.

Although extensive research now substantiates the science behind these concepts, I have chosen not to make this a textbook with dozens of references footnoted. At the end of the book, however, you will find a list of some very special authors and teachers whose ideas radically shifted my worldview. I have been very fortunate that the right people crossed my path at the right time, and that I was able to recognize them and make good use of the wisdom they brought me. These meaningful encounters are ever-present even today, and are too numerous to be noted here. However, there have been some remarkable *connectors* and *mavens,* as Malcolm Gladwell would call them, who deserve to be recognized.

More than any other person, Deepak Chopra altered my perception of the world and forever changed my beliefs about what is possible to create within it. A world-renowned authority in the field of mind-body healing, his brilliance touched my life deeply in the late 1980s. I met Deepak for the first time in January 1994 at the Chopra Center located in the L'Auberge Hotel Del Mar in Del Mar, California. A year later, I called Deepak to explore the possibility of working together to create a Chopra Center in

New York City. After many months of analysis and discussion, we decided the timing was not right for a New York or London location. When later Deepak asked if I would help create and implement the design for the new building he had purchased in La Jolla, California that was to become the Chopra Center's new home, I of course said yes. During my time working with Deepak, I met countless amazing and insightful people who in turn introduced me to other incredibly remarkable people and brilliant thinkers—among them Arielle Ford.

Arielle is the woman credited with launching the careers of Deepak Chopra, Jack Canfield, Neale Donald Walsch, Wayne Dyer, Debbie Ford, Marianne Williamson, Louise Hay and don Miguel Ruiz to name a few. Since then, Arielle has kept me connected to an ever-expanding world of new discoveries and ideas through the work of cutting-edge thinkers, brilliant authors and filmmakers—all of whom continue to enlarge my understanding of the cosmos and my place within it. It was Arielle's words of wisdom that ultimately nudged me to write this book and urged me to tell my story as a way to help others lead more fulfilling lives.

Please remember that the wisdom distilled in this book is not *the truth* . . . it is my truth. You, of course, are the one who will decide the extent to which you use this information. My deepest wish for you is that the concepts offered here will expand, improve and change the course of your life, as they have mine.

Carla Picardi
Asolo, Italy
Autumn, 2011

PART I

Being Positive

"We are only as happy as we make up our minds to be"

Abraham Lincoln

CHAPTER ONE

Attracting Positive

Being Positive Creates More Positive

From ancient scholars to 21ˢᵗ century scientists, the topic of being positive versus negative has stimulated an enormous amount of conversation, research and literature. Positive and negative states of being, we now know, affect everything from our bodies and our health to the future of our world and the universe we inhabit. Quite simply, being positive creates more positive and being negative creates more negative. Although I have believed and practiced this for years, I am still amazed every time I see evidence of it in my own life.

Lots of people claim that positive people like me live in a bubble—a *Pollyanna* type existence. This is not really accurate because it is with great intention and deliberate choice that I, and others who believe as I do, work toward holding steady in this place of positive emotions. Like everyone else, positive people can sink into a negative frame of mind. The only difference is that we use great discipline to snap ourselves back into a positive place as quickly as possible so as not to start attracting negative things into our lives.

Years ago, I had just finished a big project for Swiss Re in New York City. There was no more money coming in and the debt was piling up. Yet I knew on some deeper level that things would somehow work out for the best. In fact, every time I felt the slightest tinge of anxiety percolating inside me, I would repeat this phrase like a mantra—*"Something GREAT is going to happen!"* Because I was at a crossroads in my life, I didn't exactly know what to wish for, so I trusted that the words *"Something GREAT is going to happen!"* and the feelings they generated within me would lead me to the next step. *"I'm ready,"* I would affirm. *"Bring me my perfect life!"* By this I did not mean **the** perfect life; I meant the life that was perfect for me at that time to bring about the most expansive growth and learning.

Sonia Choquette had written a wonderful book called *Your Heart's Desire,* which I used as my guide for making this shift. I knew that I could not make the transition to the next phase of my life using a head-based strategy. Instinctively, I felt it would have to arise from a deep heart-felt desire. Guided by what Sonia calls her Principles of Creativity (which I later realized was essentially the *Law of Attraction*), I followed the three guiding rules she asked readers to commit to: 1) *travel lightly*—in other words, leave behind the way you **think** life works; 2) *take responsibility for your dream*—you created everything in your life up to this moment, and thus you have the power to create your deepest desire as well; and 3) *don't be a control freak*—you cannot jump to something new if you fear risk, injury or disappointment, because these place you in your ego, not in your heart. As a controlling perfectionist, I knew that #3 in particular was not going to be easy, and—being deeply committed to changing the course of my life—I was ready for the challenge.

With these guiding rules in mind and a deep personal commitment to change my life, I decided to pass up a couple of lucrative positions to direct controversial projects with highly volatile owners, because every cell of my body told me that this choice was not in alignment with my desires. As weeks turned into months, friends and family became very worried about me. I recall vividly one particular conversation with my mother. *"Oh Carla,"* she said, *"I am so worried about you!"* Knowing that she did not understand the depth of my conviction to shift to a life that was perfect for my next phase of growth, I stopped her mid-sentence, and in as loving a way possible I said, *"Mom, PLEASE . . . if you really love me, stop worrying about me . . . just picture something GREAT happening for me!"* By this time, I was clear about the toxic nature of worry and was keenly aware that many of my closest friends and family felt my situation untenable, and the way I was responding to it naïve. I asked them to please put aside their own fears and honor me by *"picturing something GREAT happening for me!"*

When something great *did* happen, almost seven months after I started putting my attention on *"something GREAT happening,"* people were of course happy for me, and they were also surprised that I hung in there through those dark times. One of my dearest friends said, "Wow, I know you kept saying, *'Something GREAT is going to happen!'* but who would have known it would have been something **so** great!" In that moment, the opportunity arrived that solved all my problems at once.

Although I already believed in the power of attracting what I desire into my life, attracting something *this* perfect shook my whole existence. I never expected the epiphany that followed. I was struck by a profound knowingness that *if we are capable of getting out of our own way, something more perfect than we could have ever imagined will make its way to us.* Once you know something like this, you know it in every cell of your body, and you can never again pretend you do not know it. I now owned this wisdom. *"This stuff really works!"* I thought to myself. It was all about me choosing what I desire and who I wish to be—and then just holding steady.

Back in 1997, when *"something great did happen,"* I recognized clearly the role I had played in creating that shift, and I also distinguished some helpful clues: When something is right, it is easy. It unfolds quickly and almost effortlessly, as though each piece of a pre-designed puzzle were falling into place. It had not always been this easy—possibly because I had never surrendered so fully or held steady so consciously.

How We Create Our Lives

I have often felt like I am two very separate people who seem to work well together: an ambitious, hard-driving business person who has achieved success in the outer world, and an intuitive, sensitive person who uses a combination of knowingness, faith in the order of things and discipline to remain focused on what I desire to create. Somehow both have interacted harmoniously to generate my life.

I was raised in an Italian-American Catholic home outside of Boston. My mother was an only child and my father's only sibling, his brother, became a Franciscan monk. When we were young, most family holidays and free weekends were spent with my uncle at the seminary or visiting my grandparents and other relatives, some of whom were also clergy. I realized early in life that these religious folks were just people—people who were happy one day and moody the next; people having a laugh or experiencing a moment of pain. They went to the bathroom, they had indigestion and they put their underpants on one leg at a time just like the rest of us. They were no more *speaking the word of God* than any other person. They were all just people who were doing the best they could—albeit while wearing funny clothes.

The gift this realization gave me even as a child was a certain level of compassion for the "super-person" role that many religious people are expected to play in our society, and a complete lack of intimidation for what they represented. This is not to say that I felt a lack of respect for them—in fact, I honored them deeply—and I also acknowledged their humanity. With that I understood that if a nun or a priest reprimanded me, it did not mean that *God* was angry at me too.

I consider myself a deeply spiritual person, yet even after 12 years of Catholic schools and all the familial responsibilities around Catholicism, I do not consider myself either religious or Catholic. Faith is the most profound gift I received from my early indoctrination in religion: *faith* in what is unseen in the moment, and *faith* in my ability to be unique and to resist being shamed into conformity. It also gave me a certain acceptance for things the mind cannot immediately confirm: If you can believe that a virgin had a baby and that the son was raised from the dead, you can hold steady long enough to consider other implausible concepts as well. To me, *faith* means having the ability to suspend disbelief long enough to allow something new to unfold; and a deep knowingness that everything is happening the way it needs to, even if we cannot see it at the time. Life as we know it is not *destiny*; it is a continuous unfolding based on what each of us creates moment by moment as a result of our choices.

My university degree is in architecture and design, so for as long as I can remember, I see things through eyes attuned to form and space. In my mind's eye, I can translate two-dimensional drawings into three-dimensional space and I can walk through that space I see in my mind and decide how well it will work in reality. I can see my dreams for my life in a similar way—I visualize where my life is going next—first in my mind's eye. In other words, I mentally create an image of what I desire next, not necessarily by "shoving a square peg into a round hole" but by taking a softer focus. This practice of picturing myself going through the motions in my imaginary life has brought me many wonderful real-life experiences and I have entered into each one with passion and enthusiasm. Or maybe it was the other way around: I entered into the unknown with passion, enthusiasm and a bit of faith, and then the amazing experiences unfolded. Either way, I often have felt awed by the magic of life and the feeling that anything is possible. It took me many years to discover that not everyone approaches life in this same way, yet I am certain that *if I can do this, anyone can do it.* All it takes is passion and enthusiasm.

When I graduated from university in 1977, I moved to New York City. Like Liza Minnelli, I too thought, ". . . if I can make it there, I'll make it anywhere . . ." I started as a cocktail waitress at the Waldorf Astoria—lunch duty at Peacock Alley—while doing freelance design work. I then moved on to various corporate design and facilities planning projects until I was appointed Vice President and Director of Corporate Facilities for a division of Citibank. Although I spent years working like a dog, I had job security. In those days job security meant also having "golden handcuffs"—a term used to signify the lucrative financial incentives that were given to employees to prevent them from leaving because most of the bonuses were not accessible for years. Although some viewed this as retirement planning, I viewed it as suffocating.

At 29 years old I wanted adventure, not security, so when an opportunity arose to move to London with a friend whose company was transferring him there, I decided to go too. I knew that although Citibank was not willing to transfer me to London, they would give me a leave of absence and support me in any way they could. With that and a place to live, I packed up my life in 1985 and left NYC. As soon as I arrived in London, Citibank called me to help them with a project on Jersey in the Channel Islands. Everything had unfolded perfectly, mostly because I believed it would.

A few months later, London was abuzz because an outspoken American named G. Ware Travelstead, the Chairman of First Boston Real Estate with Credit Suisse and Morgan Stanley were contemplating creating "Manhattan on the Thames" in the Isle of Dogs and calling it *Canary Wharf,* the name of the dock on which it was located. I had heard rumblings that a small team was working out of a few hotel suites at 47 Park Street. I called, introduced myself and said, "You don't know me but you may need someone like me because I can bring the U.S. corporate perspective to this project." "Come on in," was the reply. "We can use all the help we can get!" With that, I became the eighth person and the first woman executive to join this team, and was appointed the Associate Director of Design and Construction for the Canary Wharf Development.

Seven years later, after surviving the takeover by Olympia and York, and many other dramatic events, I had the honor of being one of a small group of Project Executives who had overall responsibility for the design, development and construction of Phase I: 4.5 million square feet of office, retail and infrastructure. For my role in Canary Wharf, I was awarded a Loeb Fellowship at the Graduate School of Design at Harvard University. This is a prestigious post-professional independent study fellowship with access to all of Harvard University and MIT given to 10 mid-career professionals each year who have proven themselves as leaders in what is known in architecture as the built and natural environment. I spent this year of intellectual utopia as a Loeb

Fellow focusing on the rebuilding of derelict urban areas and weaving them back into the fabric of a city.

After the Loeb Fellowship, nothing seemed quite the same. I moved back to NYC, was working on some interesting projects, and enjoying a newly purchased, lovely apartment where I would live for the rest of my life—or so I thought. Tired of moving so often, I was thrilled that for the first time in my life, everything I owned was under one roof. At the same time, I also knew that I was not living my perfect life. Seeking a project with meaning was more important than ever. I decided to take a more active role in creating my new life (with the help of Sonia Choquette that is!). I began to focus on the *something great that was going to happen* and let the cards fall as they may. By then I knew that things had a way of working out for the best. That was when, in late 1997, the *something great happened*. Little did I know that my life was about to change in just about every way imaginable.

I received an offer from Swiss Re to oversee the creation of the company's London Headquarters. Swiss Re had been my client in New York City. Swiss Re represented the type of patron that our planet needed as we entered the 21st century—socially, culturally and environmentally conscious, and I knew that whatever we ultimately created would be important. London was a city I knew well, having lived there from 1985 to 1992, so I eagerly accepted this exciting challenge.

The iconic Swiss Re building at *30 St Mary Axe* is now fondly referred to by most Londoners as the *Gherkin*. When I started the project, there was no design team in place, no design for a 40-story office building, and no planning permission. There was only a decision to make a London Headquarters happen. It was a clean sheet of paper and anything was possible.

I have to admit, this is my favorite part of the process of creating. This is the part where most people tell you it can't be done and where I get to prove it can. There were so many times when most groups would have given up or thought it too difficult; when many would succumb to doubt, protest that it has never been done before or complain that it would take too much time and money. This is the part where most investors would bow out saying, "I'm sorry; we don't fund buildings like this," and the part where planners would argue that it would be better to reconstruct what had been there before the IRA bombed the previous building on the site. This is that pivotal moment when positive attitude and vision push us forward to create something extraordinary.

As Project Director for the pre-construction phase, I was responsible for the management of the design, development and planning process. The building, designed by architects Foster and Partners, received the first planning permission in over 30 years for a tall building in the City of London and won the 2004 *Stirling Prize* for architecture. Because of its amazingly simple form of an elongated egg, the building is often chided as being phallic. I have always admired its sleek, aerodynamic shape and environmentally-progressive quality. I actually believe its soft curves and flowing movement give it a more feminine than masculine feel.

To me the Gherkin will always be a *paradigm-shifting building*. Not only did it signify the changing model of what a tall building would become in 21st century London, it also became a catalyst for change in the City of London itself by paving the way for tall buildings of architectural merit to be constructed thereafter. Most importantly for me on a personal level, it was a *paradigm-shifting building* because my experience of helping to create it changed the course of my life.

The Law of Attraction

Attracting the things we desire into our lives is really not so strange; positive people do it all the time. We often hear people say, "Wow, that was a dream come true," or, "It happened just the way I pictured it." Almost all of us have had this experience at one time or another, when something we thought about for so long and with such intense feelings of pleasure became real because we were an energetic match for our desire. This process of attracting what we desire into our lives is known as the *Law of Attraction*. It is called a *law* because there are a series of steps that must be followed in order for this process to attract into our lives that which we desire.

The essence of this law is that non-tangible energy is the invisible force that draws to us all physical things, and our ability to obtain what we desire hinges on us being vibrationally compatible to the desire itself. Of course, most of us were not taught to think about fulfilling our desires in this way, and to some it may sound like an almost alchemistical or magical method. I assure you that centuries of ground-breaking discoveries were once viewed with the same skepticism.

I live in a beautiful little hill town in northern Italy where not much has changed over the centuries. Yet, I am fairly certain that if I travelled back in time 200 years, stood near the fountain in the town square and invited the town's people to join me for a ride in a large object that was long and thin like a boat and flew in the sky like a bird, I would have been tarred, feathered and hung as a witch. Not because I would have been wrong, but because no one at that time would have understood anything about the Law of Aerodynamics. Today people get in airplanes all the time, and despite the fact that few truly understand how it works, they accept that *it works*. Two hundred years from now,

I am sure people will take the *Law of Attraction* for granted in the same way.

The challenge—if we are interested in enriching our lives—is to become more familiar with who we need to be and what we need to do to bring the *Law of Attraction* into daily use. In its simplest form it works like this: We attract what we think about and what we feel. The *Law of Attraction* does not judge or filter; it only attracts. So, if we would like to be thin but we are thinking about—and feeling badly about—how fat we look, we are unwittingly attracting to ourselves fat and more fat. Until we are able to identify our toxic feelings and deliberately shift to more positive feelings, we will only create more of what we do not want . . . in this case, fat. To make this shift, we need to slowly, gently begin to replace the negative feelings associated with being fat with feelings that are in alignment with being thin and in shape. We do this by cultivating thoughts such as *"I feel light . . . I feel healthy . . . I feel energetic . . . I feel attractive . . . I feel powerful . . . I feel in control of my life . . . I feel sexy . . ."* The goal is to reach a good-feeling place, and then **stop**. This is where discipline comes in. We have to stop ourselves from sliding into judgment, which is so typical at this point: *"but right now my clothes don't fit and I feel terrible . . . I am ugly and gross, disgusting and unattractive . . ."* Thoughts like these only serve to separate us further from what we desire. By attuning our thoughts and feelings to what we *do* desire, we begin to build the bridge that will eventually close this gap.

The illusion is that our desires exist somewhere "out there," separate from us and therefore out of our reach. But in truth all of life exists in a dynamic relationship—connected and one. This concept that we are all one and all connected is a very big topic, and we will explore its broader implications a little later. For now, let us consider the idea of everything being connected as it relates to attracting into our lives what we desire, versus attracting exactly what we do not desire.

To stay with the previous example, if we feel fat, or more specifically, if we feel badly about this perception of being fat, we hold ourselves separate from our desire to be thin and from our ability to achieve that desire. We believe it is *"not possible for us"* and our choices and eating habits reflect this belief. We then continually find ourselves in situations where we attract exactly what we do not desire—the experience of feeling fat. In other words, because we are focusing on the feeling of lacking the thing we desire, we are a vibrational match to attract that lack into our lives over and over again. If we could only remember that everything we desire is waiting for us and all we need to do to call it forth is to become compatible with its frequency, we would create more of what we desire and less of what we do not desire.

It's vital to keep in mind that the present circumstances of our lives are not proof of our worthiness or unworthiness; they do not confirm that we are unlucky, unlovable, have bad karma, or are being punished by a vengeful God. They are merely reflecting our *beliefs* about ourselves and our current feelings of worthiness or unworthiness. Like a rut that gets worn into a well-travelled path, our thoughts and feelings—repeated regularly, day after day, week after week, year after year—eventually solidify into beliefs. If we took a moment to really look at our lives, we would have to admit that most of us are pros at identifying what is "missing"; we keep our own personal score cards in most areas of our lives, constantly assessing how we are doing.

When we become aware that something in our lives is "missing"—a relationship, money, success—and we spiral into feelings of *wanting* what we perceive we are lacking, we separate ourselves from that which we desire. We cannot attract anything into our lives if we are focusing on the *wanting* of it, for this means that we know that it is absent from our lives. The same is true when we become aware that we have something unwanted in our lives, such as illness or obesity. If we see ourselves as separate from optimal health or ideal weight—as exemplified by the act of *not* wanting to be in our existing situation—we are then incapable of attracting our desired circumstances because we are focusing our attention on what is present and how much we detest it. In either case, we must start by changing our *beliefs* about ourselves. As author Eckhart Tolle often says, "We cannot change our outer reality until we change our inner reality."

We are meant to live in abundance of all that is, to be happy and live in joy, to feel totally fulfilled, and to experience perfect health, unlimited love, and overflowing financial abundance. If we truly believed that we were created in the image and likeness of a divine source, these experiences would come to us as an obvious conclusion. Over the centuries most major religions have made punishment and suffering so much a part of the way we think of ourselves that we no longer consider ourselves worthy of the abundance that is our divine birthright. In the true definition of a self-fulfilling prophecy, it is our lack of worthiness that colors our perception of what we believe we deserve. This in turn limits our ability to consider ourselves energetically or vibrationally matched to receive all that we desire. If we feel unworthy, we will attract all that we do not want simply by believing that it is the *truth*.

So, how do we shift this? We must decide that we are worthy and capable of attracting into our lives what we truly desire. Then we must vow to do whatever it takes to think positively and feel good in the presence of that desire. This means we must observe our feelings and thoughts on certain hot topics as they arise and we must be especially conscious. We must ask ourselves—*Does this thought make me feel good?*—and if the answer is *No*, then toss it out and replace it with a more empowering and positively-creative thought.

If lack of money is an issue, negative thoughts and feelings about this lack makes us feel bad about ourselves and draws more lack into our lives. Cultivating appreciation for what we do have will start to turn this around. We can begin to feel appreciation for having a place to live and some food to eat. Suspend judgment for the moment that the mortgage is late and they will be foreclosing soon and hold steady in this moment. *Did you have enough to eat today? Do you have a roof over your head today? Do you feel loved today?* By breathing in gratitude for all that we have now, we accelerate the fulfilment of our desires. We may not be thrilled about our current predicament; however, by accepting what is in this moment, we open the door for it to change.

I recently heard Esther Hicks, a *New York Times* best-selling author of four books, including *The Law of Attraction*, discussing the importance of acknowledging that, "where you are is where you are." She recounts—as a perfect metaphor for moving smoothly from one point to the next—their recent experience cruising through the Panama Canal. The water differential from one side of the Panama Canal to the other is 84 feet, or 25.5 meters. Their huge ship entered the canal to change levels, and slowly as each lock filled with water, they moved imperceptibly from one lock to the other until they came out the other side. There were no grand leaps or magic tricks that defy the laws of physics, just a smooth, steady transition. "It wasn't fast," she said, "but it was sure." Likewise, if we can hold steady in our appreciation for where we are now, we will move to the next place, even if it is not immediately discernible.

Esther and Jerry Hicks have produced some of the most easily-accessible and well-articulated explanations of the *Law of Attraction* and how it functions. They make it both easy and fun to see the simplicity in this process and to realize that we are the ones who make it so difficult to attract what we desire into our lives. We send out a desire and seconds later we start thinking about how it is not possible—and in so doing the powerful energy of our desire is negated! Desires are launched out and sucked back, over and over—it is enough to make us motion sick, or downright exhausted. Once we recognize our role in blocking the fulfillment of our desires, the process becomes a whole lot easier.

Inhale deeply and put your attention on the knowingness that your desires will be fulfilled. If you are concerned about money, remind yourself that *the money always comes*—while at the same time detaching from any desperation related to your desired outcome (this is the hard part for we who are accustomed to being in control). Breathe in those feelings that will attract financial abundance: *I feel so free when there is money! I feel so secure when there is enough money! I feel magnanimous when there is enough money to take care of everyone and everything this family needs!* When we promote and prolong these feelings of gratitude—*everything is happening perfectly the way it needs to and the money always comes*—we are sending out our pure desire to the universe.

If you find yourself reverting back to *fear*-based thoughts of desperation, anxiety or control, you can remind yourself of the famous proverb: "This too shall pass." And if the negative commentary persists . . . *the bills are piling up and there is someone calling every hour for money and I can't stand it!* . . . then look for more practical ways to keep yourself positive. It may be necessary to turn off the phone and let the mail remain unopened until this shift in awareness is complete. Each of us needs to decide how best to achieve feeling positive in each moment, knowing that the sooner we do, the more easily our desires will be fulfilled.

Remember that our only responsibility in implementing the *Law of Attraction* is to decide what we want, put our thoughts and feelings on the presence of it (not the lack of it) as already being in our lives, and then live in joy. Positive people may find this process inherently easier. Less positive people may be confronted with more frustration and suffering until they are prepared to make the choice to shift. I will tell you, however, that once you begin to see some movement in a situation where you previously believed you were stuck, it will be easier to generate and sustain these more positive feelings. As with any habit or discipline, with time, the process will get easier.

I have found it particularly effective to launch a desire out into the nothingness when I have no immediate attachment to the outcome. In fact, as I look back on all the significant shifts, changes and strides forward in my life, all were precipitated by an articulated desire, usually framed in what may seem like a whimsical phrase: *"Wouldn't it be nice . . ."* Because I was generally happy in my life at any of the moments when these desires were launched, they were sent from a place of joy rather than clouded by doubt or attachment. Even to me, my dreams always felt more like imaginative play and less like a serious and intense longing.

"Wouldn't it be nice to make it in New York City?" "Wouldn't it be nice to negotiate and manage all my own project deals?" "Wouldn't it be nice to be a Vice President for Citibank while still in my 20s?" "Wouldn't it be nice to get into the international business scene?" "Wouldn't it be nice to move from the corporate facilities side of the property business to developing buildings?" "Wouldn't it be nice to have a break from the rat race . . . maybe some intellectual stimulation?" "Wouldn't it be nice to do a paradigm-shifting building this time?" "Wouldn't it be nice to retire

at 45?" "Wouldn't it be nice to retire in Italy?" "Wouldn't it be nice to know myself as someone that could commit to a long-term relationship?" "Wouldn't it be nice to find my soul mate?" "Wouldn't it be nice to use my people skills in a different way?" "Wouldn't it be nice to teach what I have learned and support others in creating a life they love?" . . .

Are you seeing the simplicity of this? Do you get it?! These phrases that seemed like whims tossed out from my heart were broadcasting into the ether my deepest feelings and desires. Because they were not desperate pleas, they entered the atmosphere as pure, untainted desire. I was not attached to the outcome. There was no desperation in my desire being launched, only a feeling of *wouldn't it be nice* if it actually happened. Then I went on living my life, and with the exception of a few minor dramas, I was living in joy and having fun.

This process has been called putting *attention* on your desire without *attachment* to the outcome. The important part is the disconnecting of two things we normally merge together: *attention* on our desires without *attachment* to the outcome. This takes discipline. To reap the rewards we seek, we must be willing to do our part by being all of whom we need to be to allow the *Law of Attraction* to function.

The Discipline of Being Positive

For the most part, we are a society that values discipline. We go to the gym because we are fat-phobic, we work long hours in our quest for success. If we love to eat and we relish a nice big bowl of pasta or a flaky croissant, it is not a big deal. If we go for seconds or thirds, however, a little voice inside says, *"Enough . . . stop . . . this is not good for my body."* If we love to drink, we may share a good bottle (or two?) of wine with a friend, and after a certain point a little voice inside says, *"I've had enough. Any more would not serve me."* There is a natural check-and-balance system hard-wired into our bodies, designed to support us in maintaining health and equilibrium. Why is it, then, that we can indulge ourselves in negative thought after negative thought and no similar alarm bells go off inside to remind us that this type of negativity is just as hazardous to our health? I believe it is because most of the time we do not even recognize these thoughts as something we should manage or something that might be toxic.

When I present the concept that negative thoughts are in fact toxic, people who have taken the time to notice the way they have felt after engaging in this kind of thinking tend to agree. However, if our lives are filled with one negative thought after another, we may not notice them as toxic and their presence may seem simply—*normal.* Scientists say the average person has approximately 60,000 thoughts per day, around 80% of them are negative, and closer to 95% are the same thoughts looping around over and over again. Most people are surprised when I pose the question: *Why not manage these negative thoughts?* The concept of using the same discipline that makes us awaken at dawn to go for a run before work, to push ourselves away from the table when we have eaten enough or to stop drinking before we get drunk seems absurd when discussed in relation to stopping the loop of negative thoughts spinning around inside of us. Many people say, "It is just not possible."

Yes, it is. In the same way someone who is obese can lose weight or someone who is an alcoholic can quit drinking, it is possible—*if you believe it is possible.* It is a discipline, and a moment-to-moment practice. The first and most important step is to truly believe that managing negative thoughts is possible for you. After that, a few days of simply observing how often you fall prey to a pattern of toxic thoughts is very important. Just observe yourself—with no judgment.

Most of us have no idea how to simply observe ourselves or others without leaping immediately into judgment. So, the first challenge will be to separate an *observation* from the subsequent *judgment*. Here is an example: We look out the window and see that the unmarried 17-year-old girl who lives next door is very pregnant and wobbling to her car. Initially, this registers as merely an observation: *the girl next door is pregnant*. Notice how quickly we then leap into judgment: "Is she crazy?!" "Wow! What a slut!" "She never had any sense anyway!" "I suppose that kid thinks she is mature enough to bring a baby into this world!" "Why didn't she just have an abortion?" These and countless other judgments on all sides of the political spectrum seem to arise spontaneously and uncontrollably.

The first thing to acknowledge is that observation and judgment are not a package deal. Observing is witnessing that something *is what it is*; judging is jumping to a particular conclusion and assigning a meaning to what we observe. In the case of our 17-year-old neighbor, we have no idea how she feels about her situation—whether she is happy or devastated—and whatever she is going through is not ours to judge. By observing the judgments we hold regarding our neighbor, we have an opportunity to see many things about ourselves. We may glimpse our discomfort with the situation, and an almost lurching force inside of ourselves crying out to judge her. We may see also how easy or difficult it is for us to feel compassion for someone who is in the midst of a difficult situation. Compassion is a useful tool in breaking the knee-jerk connection between observation and judgment. If we take a moment to feel compassion, the urge to judge softens. Compassion helps to hold back both our impulse to judge another as well as our impulse to *judge ourselves*. It also helps us forgive ourselves when we observe how much energy we invest in toxic thoughts. Compassion moves forward the process of self-observation, which is essential for our personal growth.

After a few days of observing ourselves and how often we get stuck in this toxic loop of negative thoughts, we may also notice how difficult it is **not** to judge ourselves by what we discover as we observe our tendency toward negativity. Once we shed light on something we never noticed before, we begin to see it everywhere. Slowly this process of observation without judgment sets in motion a diffusion of heaviness and we become more and more accepting of *what is*. Once we are capable of observing our negative feelings without judgment, we can begin the process of substituting those negative feelings with more positive ones.

Our propensity to worry is another formidable pitfall to attracting what we desire, and here applying discipline can also help. The "worry" we are discussing is the insistent, anxious agonizing we do constantly, most often without recognizing we are doing it. Many of us worry about so many things in life, too many insignificant things, and far too often. It might be helpful to begin observing how often we worry and the types of worries that occupy our minds the most. It is interesting that as I write this, there is emerging a whole new body of research that claims that worrying is good for our health. However, when exploring further their definition of "worry," I discovered that it refers more to being proactive about our health and conscientious about the way we live our lives. This is not the kind of "worry" we are discussing here.

Mothers sometime think it is their role as responsible guardians to worry about their offspring, even if that offspring is 50 years old. Some even confuse worry with love. "If you love someone, of course you worry about them." My mother is a worrier. She is also a woman of strong religious conviction. I often tease her about this emotional dichotomy by asking her why she has no faith. Her response is, "Of course I have faith!" I then ask her, "Then why are you worrying???" at which point she usually shakes her head and says something like, "Oh, I don't know!" It does not strike her—just as it does not strike a lot of people—that if we really had faith in a higher power, in our own abilities, or in the concept that we are supposed to be happy, live in joy and do what it takes to feel good, we would not permit ourselves to linger in worry. Worrying is toxic. When we worry we are attracting to ourselves exactly the things we are worrying about because we are focusing on what we do not want. If something unwanted finds its way into our awareness, the best thing we can do is to let it go, cancel it from our minds and hearts by picturing the outcome we do desire and reminding ourselves . . . *everything is ok . . . everything will be fine.*

Anytime we are worrying, judging or spinning in a loop of negative thoughts, we are permitting ourselves to be manipulated *by ourselves.* Without the benefit of previous preparation, we may be incapable of stopping this downward spiral once it starts. Inner discipline is needed to snap ourselves out of these detrimental states of mind and into a more positive one, and this must be practiced. Like any exercise, the more often we do it, the easier it is and the more it becomes part of us. If we wish to attract more positive into our lives, we must begin by observing where we are, and only from there can we shift to a place of greater joy and appreciation.

Take a moment to look at your life.

- What is on your list of wanted and unwanted items?
- Where have you been attracting into your life exactly the things you say that you do not want?
- What are you worrying about?
- In what aspect(s) of your life do you feel things are not possible?

These answers will help you get a clear picture regarding: *Where am I now?*

Now, breathe . . . As you inhale, acknowledge where you are now and begin to feel compassion as you observe your present state.

- Can you accept that this is where you are now?
- Can you hold steady observing yourself without judgment?
- Are you observing any worries arising?
- Can you shift to a more positive place inside?

Make a list of what you desire, making sure to state it *in the positive*—"thin" vs. "not fat," "financial security" vs. "not poor," "rewarding career" vs. "not to be without work."

- Are you ready to launch some of these desires out into the ether? What are those deepest desires?
- Do these desires make you feel fulfilled and joyous?

Now release your desires by saying:

"Wouldn't it be nice if . . . ."

And gently release one desire after the other.

Observe your feelings as you do this process, reminding yourself that *what you are feeling* about the desires you are tossing out into the ether is what creates. Repeat this exercise until what you observe is a pure desire without any judgment attached. Think about your desires and smile. Then let it go and live your life in joy.

Remember, you do not need to know how to obtain these desires. You only need to feel good about the thought of each one being fulfilled.

CHAPTER TWO

The Role of Happiness and Appreciation

Why is Choosing Happiness Important?

There is a huge body of research that demonstrates that our emotions affect our physical bodies. Medical doctors are becoming holistic enough to ask questions about their patients' emotional as well as physical states and to correlate the two. Medical schools are now filled with students who—in the 21st century—do not consider the issue of a mind/body connection as strange. It is now a common occurrence to pick up one of the many respected medical journals and read an article on the latest research of some group of doctors or scientists who have found another way to substantiate how our immune system responds to happiness or is suppressed by anger or sadness, or even how our brain can change in response to our experiences and our DNA altered by long periods of depression. People speak of being healed from life-threatening diseases by the power of their intention to be healed, by laughter therapy or some other modality that would have sounded outrageous just a decade ago. Now we respond by saying, *"Wow, good for them!"*

Happiness helps us flourish and supports our well-being. Our emotions drive our brain activity, our respiratory, cardiovascular, nervous, hormonal and reproductive systems, and even influences which parts of our DNA get switched on and off. Happiness rewires our brains and actually makes changes in the brains of the people who experience our happiness. Over 30 years of research demonstrates that positive emotions generate higher cognitive functions, help reduce depression, and produce optimal states of health. Even the World Health Organization recognizes the profound connection between happiness and well-being, and some industrialized nations are going so far as contemplating national happiness as a factor in gross domestic product calculation. We hear it discussed everywhere—the psychology of happiness, the economics of happiness, the politics of happiness, the geography of happiness, the physiology of happiness, the genetics of happiness—and still, many of us are not convinced. Some of us feign disbelief about the role of positive feelings in our overall health and the generation of a powerful life. Others are not even sure we have a role in creating our happiness or how to go about achieving it.

Happiness is a choice. We need to decide ahead of time to be happy. Happiness and positive thoughts do not just arrive because some people are lucky and received the "happy gene" at birth. Most happy people are happy because we *work* at being happy. We place ourselves in situations that will attract happiness and we foster relationships that bring joy. We choose in each moment what is more important to us—being right or being happy. It is always a choice, and a choice anyone can make—anytime.

Happiness is discipline, an exercise, a habit, a goal. In every moment, if we choose to be conscious, we can ask ourselves:

Am I practicing gratitude and joy? Am I looking for what is good in this situation or what is missing? The *happy* we are discussing is *long-term happy* not *quick-hit happy*—which is really more ego satisfaction than authentic happiness—although that too is all part of our choice. I believe most of us innately understand the difference between *long-term happy* and *quick-hit happy*, and for the record I will give you a few examples. Having the three-scoop ice cream might give you a moment of delicious satisfaction that in a few hours may turn to regret. Having a quick affair with your best friend's wife might bring some much needed spice into your life that may translate as happiness, and you will eventually have to deal with your own feelings—if not the feelings of others—which may bring heartbreak, guilt, or shame. Being elected the president of your Rotary Club might give your ego a happy boost, while dedicating all the personal time required to fulfill this obligation may not deliver the same level of joy.

It is difficult for most of us to decipher clearly what will make us truly happy. This is in part because our ego enters the decision process with a loud voice, and nothing makes our ego happier than *immediate* satisfaction. That is why deciding ahead of time to be happy is a far more reliable strategy. We decide to be happy, *long-term happy,* when we feel appreciation for all that is and all that we have in our lives . . . and demonstrate that by living in joy. The *Law of Attraction* functions by attracting into our lives just what we need to make ourselves happy because we are launching those desires out there from a joyous place of appreciation. When we see someone in possession of whatever we desire, instead of feeling envy, we can appreciate that another has already created it, and therefore it exists as a possibility for us as well. If we wish to attract something into our lives, we need to celebrate it anywhere and everywhere we see it. This level of appreciation will call it into our lives more quickly.

Initially, it requires a reasonable amount of discipline and energy to take responsibility for our happiness and feel gratitude regularly. Most of us have never been taught how to do this, or if we have, we may be sorely out of practice. Therefore, we must be extra conscious—that means being vigilant in observing our emotions. Although we may think that we are feeling gratitude and therefore generating happy thoughts, honest self-observation may reveal that the majority of our thoughts and feelings in fact are not so appreciative or joyous. We may notice that our thoughts are filled with worry, judgment and confusion about what has transpired in our past, what we perceive is lacking in our lives presently, and what is unknown—our future.

It may be difficult for those of us who find ourselves dwelling constantly in either the past or in the future to find a method to tune our focus to *be here now*. Yet the here and now is the only place where we can feel true gratitude. So, if we are bouncing between ruminating in the past and worrying about the future, we need to start observing where we are now—literally—and without judgment. Do not judge how difficult this is or how long it is taking to stop, just observe . . . *where am I now . . . where am I now . . . and now . . . ok, where am I now.*

I have been introduced on several occasions to a powerful *present-moment centering* process involving either rooms, bubbles, circles or boxes. Use whichever shape resonates most; personally, I prefer the boxes. To start this exercise, visualize three boxes in front of you, level with your face. The box to the left of your face is your past, the box to the right of your face is your future and the box directly in front of your face is your present. If you are rehashing the past, picture yourself in that box to the left, then see yourself physically reaching your hands into that box and moving yourself into the present. If you are worrying about the future, picture yourself in the box to the right and observe yourself physically reaching into the box and moving yourself back into the present. When you ask the question . . . *where am I now* . . . you will notice exactly where you are—in which box you are residing—and you will have the opportunity to make adjustments. This process helps bring us into the present moment. It also helps each of us observe where we most often dwell before we become conscious.

After a few weeks of this, we will begin to recognize quite clearly when we are conscious, meaning when we make a choice to notice if we are holding steady in the present, or slipping into the past or the future. How we feel physically will always reveal the truth. If we feel calm and peaceful, most likely we are in the present. If we feel agitated, nervous or uncomfortable, we are not. If we are rehashing the past or are worrying about the future, then we are not in the present and we will not be able to exercise our true appreciation. There are several good meditation and mindfulness practices discussed at the end of the book that may help quiet the noise. Find one that works for you and practice daily for at least 12 minutes as a means to quiet the mind and develop the discipline to hold steady in the present moment.

Appreciation plays a huge role in happiness by enabling us to access positive feelings even when the things we desire most are not yet present. Appreciation is a muscle that in most people is usually grossly underused; therefore we need to exercise it. A lot of people complain that it is not so easy to find things to appreciate. I would argue that if we cannot, in this world of a million miracles, find *anything* to appreciate, we are not looking very hard.

In truth, even a brain that is functioning at the lowest levels is capable of this: . . . *Are you breathing? Can you see this book? Did you have the ability to walk to the kitchen this morning and enough food to make breakfast? Do you have a roof over your head? Do you have people in your life that you love and that love you? Do you have a job?* . . . Start simple—give gratitude for each breath you take . . . for the ability to move and see and hear and taste and feel and love.

Do your best not to judge the things for which you are developing appreciation: *"Sure, I can breathe but with the two packs of cigarettes I smoke each day, I will be on a ventilator soon, "* or *"Yes I have a house, and if you saw how small it is, you'd realize crawling to my kitchen is no big deal . . . and since I lost my job, I am not so sure how long I can afford to live here anyway!"* or *"Who has people who love them? The only time I hear from my kids is when they need money!"* We may laugh at the absurdity of these responses and yet this is precisely how we sabotage our appreciation workout. If we wish to be negative, we can always find something about which to complain. On the other hand, if we wish to shift the misery in our lives, we must be willing to experience something new.

Find something to appreciate, no matter how small, and truly feel gratitude for it. *"I have nice hands; I have always had elegant fingers and nice nails. I really feel good about myself when I look at my hands."* If we really cannot think of one thing about our bodies or our lives that stimulates genuine appreciation, try this: *"That is a beautiful tree; I have always loved that tree. It is so majestic and elegant. I am so fortunate to be able to see this tree so often."* Some people call this developing *an attitude of gratitude.*

Remember that being positive is all about *perspective.* The vantage point from which we choose to view our lives has everything to do with how easy or difficult it will be to attract happiness into our lives. As we begin to hone our skills of observation, we may see that our perspective may not be serving us. Then we can choose to pick ourselves up and shift our perspective, a little or a lot; by a few degrees or a full 180 degrees. We may find things look very different from this new vantage point. Many of our *stories* may no longer be relevant.

Our Stories and Their Role in Creating Our Lives

We all invent stories about ourselves that are like fables; there is some seed of truth, which we permit to grow into a *Little Shop of Horrors* plant. We tell these *stories* over and over again to ourselves and to others, and then we actually come to believe that these *stories* are true. *"I'm not good at math"* . . . *"My bosses are so stupid that it's impossible for me to care about the quality of my performance at work"* . . . *"My mother said that I am lucky that I have a good head on my shoulders because it will make up for not being so pretty"* . . . *"Women only want my money, they don't care about me"* . . . *"I cannot be faithful to anyone; it is not my nature"* . . . *"I'm not good at details; I am more a big-picture guy."* These stories are an important part of who we have come to believe we are—and they are all an *illusion*. I will discuss this concept **Our Life is Our Illusion** in greater detail later in **Part II**. For the purposes of this discussion about deciding to be happy ahead of time and cultivating appreciation to help the process along, recognizing the *stories* we tell ourselves can be very helpful.

As you consider the theme of the conversations you have with those around you—and the conversations you have within yourself—imagine that each of your stories has a headline. Have fun listing as many headlines as you can think of, and give each of your stories entertaining captions. Here are a couple to get you started: *No man ever stays with me, even my father deserted us* . . . *My wife has a new husband and I have been replaced in this family* . . . *My boss never appreciates my work* . . . *Poor me, I never have enough money to meet my needs* . . . *Nobody ever really listens to me* . . . *I am not the kind of person that does well on tests* . . . *I never get the respect I deserve* . . . *No one cares about me; I am so alone in this world* . . . *Life has always been a struggle, nothing comes easy for me* . . . *My managers are a bunch of idiots, one more incompetent than the other.* Do any of these sound familiar? Begin to observe how often you bask in the drama of your *stories*. Conversations, relationships, and entire lives are built around just these types of stories. Notice how the more you tell the story the more you make it your *truth*.

Sure, we all love a good drama . . . and these stories do not serve us. Once we recognize them for what they are—merely *stories* we have created that now define our lives—we can let them go and replace them with stories that frame us in a more positive light. We can simply ask ourselves: *Do I feel happy when I tell this story that features me as a victim? What would be a more empowering story?*

Dana spent several years of her life developing a software company that provided a tool for managing a specific area of manufacturing. After numerous problems, partners bailing out and quasi-financial ruin, a larger tech company stepped in and saved her company. The median age of the new owners was about half of Dana's. She resented these "punk kids" and hated going into the office. After a torturous six months, they offered her a half million dollars to go away. She called me crying, saying, "They fired me, they don't want me and I feel really bad!" I said, "Could we reframe this story please!? Let's try this: *I am the luckiest person in the world. My business was going under and someone stepped in to save it. I hated being there and they gave me a half million dollars to go live my life . . . and I never have to see them again! Yippee!*" Dana started laughing. "You're right, that is so true!" Needless to say, she felt much happier about the situation when she chose to view it that way.

It is interesting that most of us always seem to tell the story that makes us feel bad about ourselves, that makes us look like the loser, the one that portrays us as either the victim or the tyrant. Once we are capable of shifting our perspective, we will write a different story. We will have the power to decide: victim or victor—without making anyone else wrong or stupid. The moment we choose how we wish to frame our stories—meaning from what perspective we wish to view and represent our lives—we are beginning to attract what will unfold next in our lives, and we set in motion the course of our future. In learning to reframe the stories we tell, we ensure that the next moments of our lives will be more positive and joyous. And then, of course, the time will come when we no longer need our stories at all.

Years ago a very wise friend Hilda said to me, "Carla—let go of the stories!" I was shocked. I loved my stories. Being a bit of a ham and enjoying the art of making people laugh, I loved telling the next installment of the big drama of my life, which I built up like a comedy routine. I thought people found it captivating and entertaining, so I told it over and over until the next drama inspired the next episode. Hilda's point was that the more often I recount the drama, the more drama I created, which attracted more of what I really did not want into my life.

At first I must admit her comment seemed hurtful and it did not make sense. Then I realized that the less I recounted these stories, the less frequently these calamities seemed to occur. In the initial months, I was pleased about the diminishing drama in my life. Then I began to feel like something was missing. I noticed I had become addicted to my dramas in a certain way and I missed that feeling. I remember admitting to friends that there was a part of me that felt really boring now. If I did not recount my *stories,* I felt that there was nothing funny to talk about. Maybe I also missed being the center of attention and having the ability to entertain my friends in a way I knew so well.

Yes, my situations were funny and they were also painful; most significantly, they substantiated my belief that my *stories* about who I was . . . were *true.* At the time, I knew on a profound level that making this shift was helping me become *long-term happy.* I was letting go of the drama that I attracted into my life to prove that my *stories* were *true*. I encourage everyone to do the same.

Not all of us use our *stories* to be funny. We may use them to demonstrate how bad our life is, how terrible we have been treated, or to prove how much we deserve everyone's pity. We may also need our stories to prove how much smarter we are than everyone else and how incompetent others are in comparison. It is difficult to be happy and to stimulate positive thoughts if we are emotionally invested in being either victims of our circumstances or in proving that we are superior to everyone who crosses our path. If we are attached to the mileage we get out of blaming others—whether our boss, our ex-spouse or our parents—we are permitting ourselves to be victims and allowing this energy to set the tone for our lives. **Anytime we blame another for our situations, we give away the power we need to create the lives we desire**.

It is important to remember that the only thing we are in control of is our choices—and we are always just a choice away from our happiness. Letting go of our stories is about choosing to be happy instead of being right. We must consciously decide if we want to remain victims and lash out at others in blame, or if we are willing to take responsibility for creating happiness in our lives. If we break down the word responsibility, it simply means the *ability to respond*. The more overwhelming the situation, the more discipline is necessary to get to the place where we are able to respond and choose happiness.

Although on paper Linda has been divorced for over 10 years, she is still totally consumed in her marriage. She obsesses daily over every detail of the relationship, not only with her therapist but with anyone else who will listen to her. She lives almost entirely in her *stories* about her marriage and her divorce. Linda's *stories* "comfort" her by making her right and justifying her behavior. They give her the right to remain miserable and depressed, to feel like a victim in nearly every situation and to avoid being present in her own life and in the lives of her children, family and friends. When anyone lovingly suggests that it might be time to start living again, Linda becomes indignant, insisting that, *"You just don't understand what I am going through!"*

We all have known someone like Linda—perhaps at one time or another we have all been someone like her as well. She recognizes that she is suffering and is intelligent enough to seek relief—as long as that relief does not include her taking 100% responsibility for her role in the problems in her life. Linda is so tied to her *stories* because they allow her to continue to blame others and to remain cast in the lead role of the poor defenseless victim. Linda continues to choose being a victim almost on auto-pilot because somewhere deep inside her she believes that she is getting something more from this behavior than she would if she were to take back her power, and with it, her ability to respond to her life. Although Linda has been in therapy for years, she is no closer to seeing her role in creating her pain.

Linda is a dramatic case in point of what life is like when we allow our *stories* to consume us. We only need to change the names and the setting, and her situation might just as easily be about us or someone we know well. We all have stories about who we believe we are. Repeating them over and over further justifies our position, even if that position is one of feeling powerless and in pain. Even if our stories are seemingly positive, they are still an idealized image of who we think we are. Dissecting these tales and coming clean with ourselves that they are *just stories* we tell ourselves can be extremely powerful. By honestly exploring the relevance of our own stories, we begin to get greater insight into *who* we are being and *what* that is creating in our lives. Letting go of our stories is the first major step in healing.

Resilience and Finding the Gift

Although extensive scientific research substantiates that our positive thoughts affect our total well-being, as expressed earlier, what is not as often discussed is how being positive helps us remain substantially more resilient during bad times. Although resilience has been scientifically investigated for years, the tragedies of September 11, 2001 brought the role of resilience into the public conversation. The conclusions are not so surprising if we understand the power of positive energy. In difficult situations our perspective is often narrowed and we feel overwhelmed. Our ability to access positive emotions helps us take a broader view of the present circumstances. The more innately positive we are, the easier it is to see some ray of light in even the darkest situation.

The research demonstrates that people who respond more positively to "negative" situations do not do so because they are in denial or have their heads in the sand. Positive people are as clear as anyone about the gravity of a particular situation, and they can also see something more. They can see the remarkable human kindnesses that tragic events evoke, and are able to focus more on the outpouring of compassion, support, caring and love than the elements of loss or injustice. In essence, they recognize the *gift*!

Some of my friends tease me mercilessly about this *gift* concept. They might recount a terrible occurrence and then, in a humorous and sarcastic way, say something like, "Now, Carla, I suppose that *you* would be able to find the *gift* in this one too?!" Sometimes I do find a *gift* in what they have shared. However, it is important to recognize that the *gift* of a particular situation is often different for each one of us—and, as in all things, finding the *gift* is a matter of choice.

In every moment as we live more and more consciously, we are choosing our response to everything that transpires in our lives. We can choose to be miserable about some misfortune, and even permit it to tear us apart by the repetition of thoughts and feelings of hatred, anger and injustice. This process will begin to attract only more of the same negativity back into our lives . . . again, the boomerang.

Often people say, "I did not have a chance to choose how to respond to this. It hit me and I was immediately consumed by sadness and rage." Maybe this is true, and once we recognize that we are just a choice away from finding a more positive thought about any misfortune, we open ourselves to the possibility of making that choice. As French philosopher Jean-Paul Sartre said, *"To choose is a choice, and not to choose is a choice. Both weigh equally in the end."* Thankfully, we are the ones with the power to choose.

Even if we do not consciously recognize that we have an opportunity to make a more empowering choice, deep inside we know this intuitively. We recognize there is a moment in which the choices we make have the potential to transcend almost any situation. Years ago, I read the powerful words written by Austrian psychiatrist and Holocaust survivor, Viktor Frankl from his 1946 book *Man's Search for Meaning*:

> *"We who lived in concentration camps can remember the men who walked through the huts comforting others, giving away their last piece of bread. They may have been few in number, but they offer sufficient proof that everything can be taken from a man but one thing: the last of the human freedoms—to choose one's attitude in any given set of circumstances, to choose one's own way."*

Positive, heart-centered people are able to be much more accepting that what is transpiring—while painful—is simply a part of the vulnerability of being human. They are willing to re-enter the game of life after a tragic event because they have a strong sense of worthiness and the conviction that everything will eventually be ok. There is a level of unconditional love that arises within positive people because their own personal value allows them to be more compassionate with themselves and others, even in the midst of a tragic situation.

Years ago when we were starting construction on Canary Wharf in London, I was working crazy hours and under tons of pressure. I also had a full social life and was, as my parents would say, *"burning the candle at both ends."* I decided to learn how to meditate, took a Transcendental Meditation (TM) course and started meditating in hopes of relieving some stress. I had only been meditating for a couple of weeks when one Friday morning a colleague and I had a terrible fight; the kind of heated discussion that escalated into lots of screaming, yelling and recrimination. I remember feeling a rush of rage that was like an out-of-body experience scorching my insides. Eventually it calmed down and we both apologized but physically, I was not the same. I felt fragile and clammy, like one feels after a near-miss car accident.

That same afternoon I was in a long negotiation with a large multi-national potential client. I remember getting up from the conference table feeling very unstable and thinking I was lucky it was Friday; I could go home and rest for the weekend. As I entered my flat, I was feeling progressively worse. I peeled off my clothes and did not leave my bed for weeks except to be helped to the doctor's office. My immune system had crashed—I was unable to work for months or even function out of bed—and I never did regain the same exceptional stamina again. No one could explain what was really wrong with me. At the time I stopped eating wheat and many other things that seemed to be aggravating my immune system. It was not until several years later when I was diagnosed with celiac disease that I realized it was the gluten my body could not tolerate.

So, what was the *gift* of this? Actually, there were many. Being in bed for months, I witnessed the outpouring of kindness, compassion and love from so many friends and colleagues who were there for me in a profound way. Like a family, they stepped in to help on so many levels. It was also during that immobile time that I read Deepak Chopra's *Quantum Healing*. His wisdom changed my worldview and caused me to question everything I previously thought to be true. These amazing concepts helped me let go of so many of my preconceived notions about the separation of the mind and body, and introduced me to all the work on which this book is based. It forced me to observe my role in my illness and helped me see how I not only contributed to the illness; I created it by my choices. Even my choice to begin meditating precipitated this shift by exposing more quickly the untenable situation I had created in my life. I needed to learn to slow down, to discover how to take care of myself and to become skilled at observing the outcomes that my choices were creating in my life.

The ability to observe ourselves, and who we are being in every moment is vitally important. Stop now … and breathe consciously … it can change who we are! James Nestor says: "How we breathe really matters" in his book Breath – *The New Science of a Lost Art.* We are all capable of re-learning how to breathe correctly. If we take time to breathe deeply, even in the darkest times, we will see a little beam of light. This is our choice point, and it is with us always. We can choose to remain in the darkness—forgetting that we ever saw the tiny ray of light—or we can choose to pick ourselves up slowly and follow that metaphorical light to its source. When we do, we open ourselves to the possibility that there is something positive to be gleaned from this—and every—situation.

There is enormous wisdom and power in finding the *gift* in even the worst situations. The resilience we develop when we are faced with a tragedy is enforced when we can find something—no matter how small—to appreciate. Ultimately, positive people are able to more quickly rise up from the heaviness of a dark circumstance, regain their balance and find their ability to respond. As we recognize that every tragedy is woven from a complex web of emotions, we are more easily able to find the ones that carry joy and are more likely to bring healing more quickly.

In January several years ago, my husband Goffredo and I went to Sweden to visit dear friends and attend a weekend seminar they were holding in a small town about an hour from Uppsala. On the Saturday evening after the first day of the seminar was complete, my husband and a few others decided to go out for a walk in the dark before dinner. Fifteen minutes into the walk, Goffredo slipped on the ice and within a nano-second, he was on the ground. Being a medical doctor, he knew the minute he tried to stand up that his femur was broken at the horizontal part before it enters the hip joint. A series of events followed to get him from the place on the road where he slipped to a local hospital and then to Uppsala University Hospital, where he underwent surgery. We spent the next week in Uppsala, he in the hospital and me nearby in a beautiful home with friends. Apart from the pain and inconvenience caused by the event, we were stunned by the outpouring of compassion, kindness, love and hospitality we were given.

We could have moaned about our terrible misfortune and what a total pain it was to be inconvenienced in this way. Instead we embraced the *what's done is done* attitude and really allowed ourselves to see the *gifts* we were given by so many people—some of whom we knew and many we had never met. Everything went so smoothly it was almost magical. We even had a little insurance policy from our bank, which paid for absolutely everything, including sending a nurse from Italy to Sweden, and arranging for ambulances at both airports to help my husband get safely and comfortably back into our home. We often laugh about that week spent in Uppsala and say what a lovely time we had . . . too bad he had to break his femur for us to have experienced that much joy!

Our ability to recognize kindness and to truly feel gratitude does more than enhance our appreciation for all the good that surrounds us. It also reinforces our immune systems, builds our resilience in times of tragedy, and places us in the warmth of positive emotions and *love*. Yet unless we have been exercising discipline around being positive, when a heartbreaking event transpires we may find ourselves incapable of snapping into action and finding something to bring us peace, if not joy.

Somehow, we have developed a warped notion: When a tragedy happens, we believe we have an obligation to dive in and be upset or worse, to be angry, and downright nasty. We feel it is our duty to join the ranks of the suffering, to remain somber, to fuel the flames of anger and resentment, and instigate a pity party of depression. None of this—in any way—is helpful. It does not serve us personally to add any negative feelings to the mix, nor does it serve the situation as a whole. No amount of sadness can shift sadness, no amount of anger can shift anger, and no amount of hatred can shift hatred.

If an incident happens that we define as bad, the most powerful thing we can do is send compassion and *love* and look for something beautiful. To some of us this might sound seriously wimpy and totally useless, especially if we perceive the misfortune as something that *has been done to us*. We want to get angry and get even. We want to load and discharge a few rounds. We want to show others who is boss and that we are right. Even if it is a global event, we want to participate in the solidarity of the moment and feel the outrage. We want to vent by ranting and raving against anyone who might be involved and we make it our mission to get them back.

Why is it so difficult to recognize the brutish nature of this response in our moment of rage? Can we not see the *moment* as just one moment in a continuum of events that led up to and contributed to the creation of this moment? Can we not remember also that *every action has a reaction* and there will be events after this that will contribute to how situations like these may unfold in the future? Inevitably, we the individual and we the collective have had a role in this event, otherwise we would not be the ones bearing witness to it. We have a role in everything that happens, even if it is as simple as our need to witness our own reaction to the event. Sometimes we are blind to our own propensity to do things that could result in an equally devastating incident. Who we choose to be in these powerful moments provides much insight into ourselves; entering a negative state guarantees that we will be affected on a much deeper level.

Feeling good is our most important responsibility in creating the life we desire. Being positive activates the powerful *Law of Attraction* and attracts into our lives what we desire. We have discussed that positive feelings enforce our immune systems and give us greater resilience in difficult moments. From this it follows that we must find a way to extricate ourselves as quickly as we can from the onslaught of negativity and shift into a more positive place.

Sending *love* is our magic wand. Sending *love* to a bad situation diffuses its ugliness and removes us from the mire. Sending *love* to a person unlocks their resistance, for beneath all behavior is nothing but the need to feel loved. Sending *love* releases the hold our egos have on us and allows us to see everything more clearly. So, how can we do this when we are caught up in hatred and rage? . . . Breathe . . . and remember that no amount of hatred, sadness or anger will do anything but add more hatred, sadness and anger to the situation. The fastest way out of the heaviness is to breathe deeply and send loving feelings.

Take a moment to observe yourself as you read and respond to these questions:

- How would you describe your level of happiness?
- How often is it more important for you to be right than to be happy?
- When have you confused *quick-hit happy* and *long-term happy* and what did you learn from the repercussions?
- What connections have you noticed between your level of happiness and your overall mental and physical health?
- What stories do you tell yourself that might be keeping you stuck in an unhelpful pattern of victimhood or blame?
- When doing the *present-moment centering* process, in which box do you most often find yourself—past or future? What emotions are holding you there? Shame? Worry?
- What are three things that stimulate immediate appreciation in you and would be most effective to pull you back into the present moment?
- How easy is it for you to find things to truly appreciate when a tragic event takes place in your life? What are some of the *gifts* you have received?
- Have you ever been caught up in the hatred, sadness or anger of a situation? What finally broke the spell? Are you able to see any *gifts* in that situation, even today?
- Do you feel uncomfortable when I use the word *love*—as in *send love* to a tragic situation? What does *sending love* mean to you?

The more honestly we observe ourselves and our feelings about everything—including answering these questions—the greater chance we have to make different choices about who we are being in every moment. The more closely we observe ourselves, the more conscious we become and the more committed we will be to observing ourselves.

Are you willing to commit to the following concepts?—

"I commit to . . .

- Being happy by choosing to be happy over being right and by looking for what is good about each situation
- Observing *"where am I now?"* as often as possible, and shifting into the present moment by finding something to appreciate as soon as I notice that I am either in the past or the future
- *Be Here Now* by being prepared with at least three things that I can immediately appreciate the second I notice that I am not in the present moment
- Finding at least one *gift* in any tragic situation from my past
- Looking for new things every day that will enhance my appreciation for all that I am and all that I have in life
- Learning a mindfulness or meditation practice and doing it for at least 12 minutes per day

CHAPTER THREE

What's Love Got to Do With It?

Love and Fear

There are two basic human states of being, *Love* and *Fear*, and all our emotional states fall within one of these two categories. When we speak about *love*, we mean all the emotions that empower us, such as joy, peace, kindness, serenity, understanding, patience, compassion, and forgiveness, to name a few. When we discuss the category of *fear*, we refer to all the emotions that create resistance and disconnect us from ourselves and from the source of all energy. *Fear* emotions include envy, anger, stress, anxiety, intolerance, judgment, resentment, hatred, jealousy and greed.

All emotions in their purest form—meaning at the instant we feel them—are a perfect expression of our being. The moment we acknowledge the feeling as an emotion and articulate what it is, we enter either into a place of empowerment that gives us the feeling of being connected, or a place of disempowerment that creates resistance. Most of us cannot distinguish the nano-second when this happens, and by the time we recognize the emotion and put a thought on it, the emotion has already begun to affect us one way or another.

Although we are complex beings, we can only truly occupy one of these basic human states at any one time. When we are residing in any expression of a *fear*-based emotion, we cannot also be in a place of *love*. At any given moment we are either operating from *fear* or we are operating from *love,* but never both simultaneously. If we choose to shift out of a *fear*-based feeling, we must create some degree of emotional access to the state of *love*.

I first learned the basics about this *Love* and *Fear* concept from Neale Donald Walsch. When Arielle Ford introduced me to Neale at her wedding celebration party hosted at the home of Deepak and Rita Chopra, I shook his hand for so long and with such appreciation that at one point he looked down at his hand and me in a pleading way until I released my grip. I had read and listened to his *Conversations with God* series so many times that I could lip-sync the words of God. More importantly, the way he described *Love* and *Fear* resonated so powerfully within me that I began to view everything as being a reflection of either the presence or the absence of *love*.

Instead of judging people as evil beings or doing nasty, unethical things, I started to see these for what they were—simply choices based in *fear.* I also began to observe myself to see if my response to a given situation was based on *fear* or *love*. I would ask myself more regularly *"where are you coming from in this moment?"* and the question referred specifically to if I was coming from a place of *love* or from *fear*. Over time I discovered that if I even needed to ask this question, it was pretty certain that I was in a place of *fear.* With that answer I could then distinguish which *fear*-based emotion I was expressing (for example anger, anxiety, intolerance, judgment). With this awareness, I could consciously make a shift from the *fear* emotion to a *love* emotion. The real challenge is to remain in a *love* emotion as often as possible because from this place of *love*, we are totally connected to all the power and knowledge that exists in this universe and beyond. From a state of *love* we are attracting health, happiness and abundance. We are strengthening our immune systems and radiating joy to all.

When we are in a *fear* emotion we are totally on our own— meaning we are in our heads, not our hearts, repeating one of those toxic mental loops we all know so well. We are going round and round in our ego, driven by some persistent thought. Something may have triggered a feeling of insecurity or anger, and with that, we remember all the other times when this person or situation made us feel this way, how frustrating it was and how powerless we felt.

We use the expression *we are on our own* because in the state of *fear* we have no immediate access to our higher consciousness or deeper wisdom. When we are in our heads in this fragmented state, we are also disconnected from our more sophisticated cognitive functions, such as reasoning, tolerance, and understanding. We are spinning in our ego, judging and needing to be right. If we want to get out of this discomfort, we must drop our resistance and make a different emotional choice. We must choose a *love*-based emotion to dissolve this state. If we feel angry or wronged, we must challenge ourselves to find some drop of kindness, compassion or forgiveness. The more often we choose a *love*-based feeling over *fear*-based feelings, the easier they are to access and the more peaceful we feel. It is only from this place of peace that we can begin to take back our power and feel appreciation for ourselves for having stopped our *fear*-based tailspin and re-stabilized our bodily systems.

This concept of *stabilizing bodily systems* may sound like something straight out of a science fiction spacecraft drama; and it is a great metaphor for what happens. Our bodily systems—respiratory system, cardiovascular system, immune system, hormonal system, endocrine system, nervous system and so forth—all receive a powerful jolt from *fear*-based thoughts and feelings, which disconnect us from our bodies, our higher cognitive functions and from the source energy that sustains us.

One of the more entertaining ways to think about this process is to imagine that *source energy* is like the World Wide Web, only on the scale of the multiverse (meaning multiple possible universes) and holds *all that is* together. We are each our own stand-alone computer that has the option to connect to the multiversal Web, and our port of connection is through our heart via a *love*-based emotion. When we are caught in a place of *fear*, we are automatically disconnected from the Web and function on stand-alone mode. Of course, unless our whole system has crashed, we still have access to whatever information is already in our computer—if we have the presence of mind to find it, that is. Most of the time, however, the state of *fear* that caused the disconnection also generates extreme mental frustration and emotional meltdown, and consequently, none of our systems function correctly. If and when we recognize the problem—that we have disconnected—we have the option to choose to shift to a *love*-based emotion. Doing so instantly restores our connection to *source energy*, where we have access to all the wisdom, knowledge and clarity *that is*.

Each of us can decide for ourselves by which name we choose to call what I refer to as *source energy*. I feel comfortable using this term to describe *all that is* in this universe and beyond; for all that we know today and all that is still unknown. By whatever name you call it, *source energy* is the power that generates and maintains the life force. It is the same energy that divides cells, creates solar systems, and grows everything from the hair on our bodies to the crops in our fields. Some people refer to this as God or as a specific name of a god that implies this all-powerful energy. Others choose to de-personify this energy, and remove it from any religious significance while at the same time acknowledging the presence of a unifying energy that is all love and all knowledge and all wisdom. When we come from a magnanimous and loving place within ourselves, we are making a connection to this source— what we shall refer to from here out as *source energy*.

Love, Fear and Leadership

Leadership is an activity, performed by an individual, so who we are being while performing this activity has everything to do with how successful we will be as leaders. At a certain point in our careers when we have amassed enough experience, we naturally become proficient at the *doing* part of our jobs; most aspects of our work can be done without much conscious thinking and anything we may not know how to do specifically, we can figure out a way to accomplish. Most of us have the doing under control. The subtle and profound part of our learning comes from who we are being in relationship to others while we are performing this activity called *leadership*. Few of us are born leaders. Leaders are created through discipline, vision, wisdom, self-reflection, compassion and constant consciousness.

In every moment of our lives we are given the opportunity to be leaders; in our families, in our work, and in our communities. Leaders are not to be confused with authority figures. We do not need to be the person in charge to be a leader. We are exercising leadership every day on numerous levels, often without realizing it. We are exercising leadership when we take 100% responsibility for *who* we are being in every moment, and when we are truly able to respond and not react. We are exercising leadership when we are in the present moment, when we are acting from our hearts and from a place of *love*.

We are exercising leadership when we set the tone for any given interaction, relationship or project and when we make a conscious choice to hold steady in that tone. Unless we take full responsibility for who we are being in each moment and make the appropriate choices that support it, we will forever be at the mercy of the tone set by another person or another situation. When the tone has been set by another, and we do not recognize what is unfolding before us, we feel like unwitting victims of the situation. We blame the person or the situation instead of stepping back to see our role in this dance and considering ways of altering it. We are sucked in, swept away, and spinning out of control. At moments like these, when we have lost our footing, we are in a place of *fear*.

This concept of losing our footing was never demonstrated to me more clearly than in a critical moment during the planning approval process in the City of London for the Gherkin. It was February 2000 and we had just walked out from a Planning Committee meeting at the Great Hall in Guild Hall. The meeting had not gone in our favor and I felt shattered. We had worked so hard for this moment. The negative feedback we just received made our impending planning permission and all the new requirements we needed to complete seem hopeless and impossible to attain. The heaviness of the moment shook the joy out of me and launched me into a place of *fear*. To make matters worse, I was attached to a particular outcome: I wanted to see the building under construction soon so I could move on to my new life. My whole future was attached to getting this done *now*.

As hard as I tried, it was impossible to muster my usual positive can-do mentality. We all had agreed to reconvene that afternoon and when I entered the room, I guess it was obvious that I was not my usual self. One of the guys on the team said, "Carla, you're supposed to be the positive one! We rely on your belief that this is possible. If you are going to give up then we should all go home." I noticed for the first time the expressions on the faces of the team looking at me. I was shocked—like a glass of cold water was thrown in my face—I woke up! I said that he was absolutely right, and in that instant, I inhaled deeply and shifted my energy to a place where I could appreciate *how much great work we pulled together already* and *what we achieved so far*. Then, somehow with that newfound surge of appreciation, I found some peace in knowing that we would be successful soon enough. I recognized that in this powerful exchange I simply did not have the *luxury* to be sad or depressed. My role in that moment was to set the tone and hold the energy that would help the rest of the team believe it was possible.

I am forever thankful for that intervention and for the courage it took to deliver it. Often in the heat of the moment we are incapable of seeing ourselves clearly. When we least expect it, another may hold up the mirror and in an instant, we see ourselves. What we do with that reflection, of course, is always our choice. Incidentally, six months later we did, in fact, receive planning permission.

Most of us know by now the types of situations that have the power to suck us in before we even know what hit us. Sometimes they are unique situations, like the one I recounted above. Other times they are recurring knee-jerk reactions, and even though we know they are coming, we cannot seem to avoid them. We often say things like, *"she just presses my buttons!"* We use the analogy of *pressed buttons* because our reaction is usually so automatic and so intense; it feels as though someone has tripped a wire or flicked a switch—and off we go.

We may vow never to let it happen again. We swear that we will be prepared next time for what we knew was coming this time.

And next time—in fact, time and time again—we get caught. Different situation, different person, different day, only who we are being remains the same. As long as we are committed to thinking that some*thing* or some*one* is to blame for our buttons being pushed, we will never find a way out of this problem.

Any time we blame another, and any time we feel like victims, we are in a state of *fear*. Our *fear* then blocks our ability to see anything clearly and to respond in the way we have planned. We may have rehearsed this over and over in our minds, specifically for this type of situation, preparing for when *that* person presses *this* particular button. Unfortunately, rehearsing a response and **being the response** are two totally different things. We rehearse what we would *like* to do in these situations in our heads, and we think this will control our reactions when the situation arises, but we cannot manage in our heads a situation that is initiated in our hearts.

When something or someone presses our buttons, we feel attacked, and within a split second we become incapable of responding just when it would serve us the most. Without prior training, the course we set in motion may even render us babbling fools or raging maniacs—indicating the depth of the psycho-physiological reaction being triggered within our own bodies. Instead of recognizing that this drama is all happening within us—and humbly acknowledging our total lack of preparedness—we lash out in blame and react like a victim of what just transpired. In this moment we are demonstrating the very antithesis of leadership.

When someone does something that *pushes our buttons,* we feel this discomfort first in our heart—which we might refer to as the mainframe of our body's computer system. The heart plays a key role in sending messages to our brain. Since our heart is regulated by our emotions—and in this particular moment we feel attacked—our heart responds first to this impulse and instantaneously sends a *fear* message to the brain. Understanding this heart-brain connection may help us move toward a different response.

Since 1991, Doc Childre and the team at the Institute of HeartMath® have been documenting how our conscious involvement in our emotional responses can reduce stress, build resilience and optimize our personal performance. Their state-of-the-art wisdom, research and development related to the heart-brain connection have been instrumental in training many individuals and organizations to understand how our brains and bodily systems function while under stress and how we can make conscious choices to hold steady in these situations.

I met Doc Childre, Deborah Rozman, Howard Martin, Rollin McCraty and the remarkable people at HeartMath® through Brian Hilliard, Arielle Ford's husband. Brian is a unique man who is secure in his existence and capable of a deep level of care and devotional love, which he demonstrates toward virtually all individuals—known and not known. Many of the heart-based principles that Brian lives by exemplify the wisdom of his friend Doc Childre. When I first met Brian he told me about the amazing work HeartMath® was doing and connected me to their books and research. When we were in California in 2006, Brian organized a trip out to the Institute of HeartMath® so that I could really understand the magnitude of their work. The time we all spent together at *camp* with Doc touched my life deeply. It left me with a much greater understanding of leadership and my role in creating and supporting the world around me.

The essence of the HeartMath® philosophy is the heart-brain connection, and how and why the heart affects our brain, which they see as the key to improving our performance on multiple levels. If we took a moment to look at the human brain in some detail, we would see that there are three main structural regions, each responsible for different levels of control. Our 1st Brain or brain stem (which includes the medulla and hypothalamus) deals with some basic survival instincts, such as the need to eat, drink, and reproduce. Our 2nd Brain (which includes the amygdale, hippocampus, thalamus, and pituitary) deals with mid-level control functions where basic emotional information, such as maternal love, memories, fear, anger, hindsight, and our primordial fight and flight response is processed. Our 3rd Brain (which includes the isocortex, frontal and temporal lobes) controls our higher cognitive functions, such as language, creativity, self-reflection, foresight, complex problem solving, and our ability to choose appropriate behavior and evaluate the consequences of our actions. Our 3rd Brain controls roughly 80% of our brain functions.

When this message of feeling *attacked* is sent from the heart to the brain, the 3rd Brain—where virtually all of our higher cognitive functions take place—shuts down. An alarm goes off and the announcement is made: *"Systems under attack, systems under attack . . . prepare to make a decision for fight or flight. 1st and 2nd Brains, prepare to take control!"* Within seconds, our higher cognitive functions close down and we instantly witness the deterioration of our most vital skills. Our problem-solving capabilities are inhibited; we are significantly less effective in making decisions; our listening is impaired and our creativity is blocked. In other words, most if not all of the skills we need right now, *especially now*, are not available to us! We are blocked. We are out of control, caught in a downward spiral. We have returned to our primordial selves, and we are fighting for our lives.

To a trained scientist this might sound like an over-simplification of a series of intricate biological processes, and it is intended only to describe a complex series of events in an easily understandable format. In essence, there will always be some *person* or some *thing* to press our buttons as long as we have buttons to press. Once this process has been unleashed, there is little we can do to stop this chain of events. This is one of the main reasons why we feel so frustrated, helpless and stupid in these circumstances.

What we can do to manage these awkward experiences is to learn to be different in the moments leading up to these situations. There is a substantial body of research that demonstrates how we can diffuse these primal reactions by practicing how to become more calm or heart-centered; that is to say, by functioning more often in a conscious state of *love*. Our work as leaders and as evolved individuals is to know ourselves and be 100% responsible for who we are **being** in every moment . . . no excuses, no blame and no judgment, even of ourselves.

The Institute of HeartMath® has developed practical, heart-based tools and exercises to enhance health, performance and well-being. These tools are particularly effective to prepare for stressful occurrences in our daily lives, as individuals and as leaders. The *Freeze-Frame*® process has been proven highly effective in preparing our bodies physically for remaining calm during perceived attacks—because it generates almost immediate physical changes in our bodies, and because this quick shift to a heart-based emotion creates neurological changes that support physical systems stability.

The *Freeze-Frame*® process works like this: First we must take an immediate time-out from the situation; disconnect from all thoughts and feelings, drop our focus to the area around our heart, and simply feel our breath coming in through our heart. Then we must find and focus on a joyous thought, something that truly resonates with us specifically, something that the moment we think of it, makes us smile. To each of us this peak sensation will be different; *the sun setting over our favorite beach . . . the smile of a loved one . . . seeing for the first time our newborn child . . . snow falling in huge flakes into our hand . . . winning our first race.* Whatever your blissful moment is, feel it, inhale it, and fix the image in your senses. This is your ticket to peace. See this moment frozen in time, encapsulated, like freeze-framing a film, and let the resonance of this beautiful moment fill every part of your body as you inhale it.

For most people it is difficult to generate appreciation on demand without practice, so using this *Freeze-Frame®* process will get our *love*-based emotions flowing. Remember that it is not simply a mental image of this memory; it is the emotions of bliss associated with this memory that will start this process moving. Inhale this blissful moment and let it wash over you.

As we begin to practice this process, profound physiological changes begin to occur. As our breathing continues, coherence is increased in our respiratory system, meaning integration and synchronization are taking place. This synchronization of the rhythms (in this case, of the body's systems) is called *entrainment*. Entrainment is a miraculous progression because it begins to modify the rhythms of all our systems to create greater coherence. When we experience cross-coherence of related systems, such as our cardiovascular system and our respiratory system, other systems become entrained and fall into coherence. Ultimately, we experience psycho-physiological or global coherence. In this state we have full access to optimal health, physical energy and cognitive performance.

Regularly practicing this *Freeze-Frame®* process is the key to enjoying global coherence. This is the discipline part, to breathe in this blissful moment regularly each day and focus on it as often as we can. We must be exercised, fit and prepared so that our bodily systems will not be sucked into an emotional reaction that disappoints us when our *buttons are pressed*. Performing this *Freeze-Frame®* process regularly will prepare us ahead of time to be different. When someone or something *presses our buttons*, we will already be in a much more coherent state and in a much better position to initiate the *Freeze-Frame®* process. In that split second, instead of the message of *fear* being sent from the heart to the brain, we will have the opportunity to hold steady while keeping our higher cognitive functions performing in an optimal way.

As we have explored, when *fear* triggers our fight-or-flight response, this condition is communicated to every cell in our bodies—our muscles tighten into knots and our immune system receives a hit, which some scientists say takes hours from which to recover. Fortunately, the reverse is also true; when we feel harmonious and in balance, our immune system is enhanced; we experience higher brain function and we can see possibilities where we previously could not. The *Freeze-Frame®* process helps us to hold steady even when we are outside our normal comfort zone. It encourages greater clarity, and allows us to be more fully present when observing, listening, intuiting and responding. Standard relaxation techniques, while beneficial, do not engage the heart and stimulate coherence—it is the elevated level of *appreciation* that stimulates coherence. The more we practice this *Freeze-Frame®* process, the easier and faster we can make the shift.

The human brain has an amazing ability to change in response to our experiences, both real and imagined. The rearranging of neurons and the changes in the organization and function of their networks is called neuroplasticity. Scientists are discovering more information daily about how our brains adjust in response to new situations and new experiences by making new connections.

Exercises like the *Freeze-Frame®* process and other methods of mindfulness and meditation help to develop our capacity to remain calm outside of our comfort zone and create new connections or pathways in the brain. We also create new pathways when we visualize living the lives we desire and doing things that bring us pleasure, even if those things have not arrived yet. Through the discipline of practicing these processes and using visualizations, we are physically changing our bodies and minds and creating noticeable changes in our outer world as well.

We are All Things . . . We are That Too

If, despite sincerely and regularly practicing our *Freeze-Frame®* process, we continue to feel these illogical moments of uncontrollable frustration and outbursts of rage, we may want to look more closely at what is driving us crazy, literally. If we still find ourselves incapable of holding steady when some person or situation is *pushing our buttons*, then we need to explore what is actually going on inside us. We are more than likely struggling with our *shadow*.

Our *shadow* is everything we do not want to be, and is responsible for the sabotaging behaviors that we deny we possess. It is our shadows that act out in rage, blame, withdrawal or vindictiveness in those moments when our *buttons are pushed*. These parts of ourselves are extremely hard to face. In fact, we prefer to disavow ownership of them altogether. Often, we do not even feel like it is a part of us; it is as if some evil being has temporarily possessed our body, mind and spirit. However, as long as we repress or deny the existence of our *shadow* we will never overcome shame, duality and conflict, or reach a point of feeling whole and worthy enough to create the life we truly desire.

If we do not yet understand why we react as we do, or how we can spiral so easily into arrogance, victimhood or inexplicable rage, it might be helpful to explore the work of Debbie Ford. Debbie is an internationally-recognized expert in the field of personal transformation and has written extensively about the dark side of the human psyche, otherwise known as the *shadow*. Her astoundingly powerful body of work has helped millions uncover, own and heal the parts of ourselves we have hidden a long time ago.

Debbie Ford was one of the first people that I met through Deepak Chopra during my time in La Jolla, California and she immediately became a friend and mentor. Debbie was part of the Chopra Center team where she was teaching, coaching and leading her highly-acclaimed *Shadow Process* workshop. Debbie has a remarkable ability to hold a mirror in front of each participant, and the fierce courage to shine a light on the exact issues one least desires to see. When we can look at all the things we hate in others (not just the parts we like) and acknowledge that we possess those traits or qualities too, we are moving toward embracing our wholeness. The more we own all of who we are—the gentle and the brutal, the beautiful and the ugly, the kind and the nasty, the polite and the rude, the generous and the stingy—the greater propensity we have to choose who we would like to be in every moment. The alternative is to feign ignorance each time embarrassing traits pop out of us when we are least prepared. Summoning the courage to take ownership of the very traits we are loathed to acknowledge comes bearing a very useful gift: we gain the ability to *use* this trait, deliberately and appropriately, when and as we choose.

The Shadow Process workshop was one of the most powerful things I have ever done. For a perfectionist like me, even the idea of having a *shadow* implied a level of imperfection with which I had trouble dealing. Through Debbie I have learned so much about the importance of owning and embracing all that I am—darkness and light, imperfections included. She taught me how to say . . . "*I am that too*" and apply it to all the traits I judged as unflattering and painful to own. Then she showed me the gift that these traits actually gave me.

Being a perfectionist has its dark side, and it has also served me well. It drove me to work hard and dedicate myself to getting things done the "right" way. It brought me success at a young age, pushed me to be all that I could be and helped me attain the life that I desired. By embracing rather than resisting this part of me, I can now use *being a perfectionist* when it truly serves me and not simply to torture myself or others. Debbie's books and lectures have been my companions on so many long journeys, and the sound of her voice will always remind me to accept all of who and what I am.

Exploring our dark side or *shadow* helps us uncover, own and heal parts of ourselves we have hidden a long time ago. If we cannot celebrate our darkness, we will never fully appreciate our light. In the workshop, Debbie asks participants to make a list of the behaviors that we see in others that really push our buttons. Then she asks a powerful question: *What kind of person would engage in this behavior? What is it about this behavior that sends us into disgust or rage?* We know we are on the right track in compiling our list if—when confronted by any of these qualities—we feel a visceral reaction that compels us to rant on and on about them. When we look at this list, we may feel a bit righteous, we may be nodding our heads thinking: "yes, these things are really terrible" . . . or . . . "the kind of people that would display this type of behavior are really disgusting."

The fascinating thing is the characteristics that give us the most charge, send us into orbit and drive us crazy, do so because we are not willing to see our propensity to be exactly the same. That list is our dark side, the qualities in ourselves that we reject, disown, and deny. We do everything to hide these traits from ourselves and others by creating a persona that is quite the opposite.

Katie was a tall woman with a booming voice who went to great lengths to portray herself as sweet, polite and gentle. When she spoke of herself she referenced a person who was the epitome of a well-bred, soft-spoken, highly-educated woman. In reality, she was bossy, overbearing, outspoken and always had to have things her way or else she was not interested in participating. She had lost many friends over the years because of this behavior, which she dismissed by saying, "Oh he (she) always needs to do things his way . . . it got too boring!" If you asked Katie what traits in others drove her crazy she would say, "I hate bossy people who always have to decide how things will be done!" She could not see that she was exactly the same and she was projecting these traits on others to demonstrate how she was the victim of these situations.

When we started working together, she could not understand what the purpose was of exploring what she described as the "distasteful qualities of other people," and could not see what this had to do with her. Nonetheless, she made her list, and it was no surprise: Katie hated people who were bossy, controlling and overbearing, and lamented over and over how annoyed she becomes when others demonstrate these qualities. Even though this discussion itself was magnifying these very qualities, Katie still was not willing or able to see her behavior in the situations of her life as anything but "appropriate." Finally, I brought up a few occasions at which I was present, in which I described a situation where the person was rude, bossy and overbearing. She agreed vociferously until I said quietly, "If I recall, that was you in these situations." There was total silence. It was only then that Katie said, with her hand over her eyes, cringing ". . . but I hate being that way! Did I really do that . . . and in such a rude way? My mother did things like that, and I remember feeling humiliated and furious at her arrogance!" Once Katie was able to see that this was not just a one-off moment but a common occurrence in her behavior, she was able to get closer to seeing herself clearly and saying, *"I am bossy, overbearing and downright rude!"* until she meant it.

When we can own all of what we are—even our so-called "worst" qualities—we can begin to look for the *gift*. In Katie's case, the *gift* of these traits is that sometimes she really needs to be bossy and overbearing. When there is a terrible crisis and everything is out of control, there is no better person to step in and get things back on track. Once Katie owned the totality of herself, she no longer needed to put on the sweet-polite act when it would serve her better to be bossy and in control. This new clarity helped Katie fulfill one of her deep desires. The funny thing was Katie had always wanted to travel to crisis spots around the world to help and she thought that maybe she was not cut out for it because she was too soft-spoken and polite to make an impact. Now that she sees herself more clearly, she is living a different life and using *bossy* and *overbearing* more often when it serves her and much less when it does not.

If we do not believe that we have a dark side, all we need to do is ask the people with whom we spend a substantial amount of time: our families, our partners, our colleagues or an assistant. They know—they have seen it in action. The only person that is not willing to see the situation clearly is *us*. It is obvious to others we are projecting; it is just not easy for us to see. When we add our own *shadow* issues to others' unexplored *shadow* issues, there is the potential of creating a *shadow* cocktail in all our encounters—where each side is convinced it is the other person's issue.

When we disconnect from feeling any one of our more vulnerable, imperfect traits, we are essentially numbing all expressions of emotion in our life. We cannot numb our shame without numbing our joy as well because they are part of the same emotional spectrum. We begin to lose our ability to feel any emotion and then we go searching for something, anything to make us feel, and not feel, all at the same time. We overeat, drink, and indulge in deviant sex as well as use and abuse all kinds of both legal and illegal drugs, all in an effort to anaesthetize our shame, and all the while deadening our propensity to feel our happiness as well.

When we separate ourselves from any part of ourselves because we feel shame, because we feel disgust, because we do not want to be that way or to think those thoughts—we give up control over that behavior. It is almost like placing that behavior *under separate management* and no longer taking responsibility for its daily operations. It soon becomes a secret operative working undercover within us and even we do not recognize its presence. The effort of hiding this behavior from ourselves and others (even though they usually know anyway) sucks our creativity, authenticity and joy. The more shame we feel about this trait, the more we hide it until finally we can hide it no longer. We explode and do the unthinkable.

The media loves playing up these true stories of famous people caught in a *shadow* incident because they are so outrageously astounding. When we see clearly the juxtaposition of the image that these famous people have carefully projected and what their crime has been, it would be almost laughable, if it were not so sad. A blatant example of the effect of not owning our *shadow* was shared with me recently.

A colleague's brother was perceived as a highly ethical accountant working for a large religious organization. He was married with children and seen as a *pillar of society*. Everyone highly respected him and said he was so sweet and such a pleasure to work with. Even the women in the office said he would always bring them coffee, doughnuts and special treats. When government officials surrounded his home office, they did not have the same opinion. They had caught him red-handed with the computer on which he just made a date to meet some woman and her 10-year-old daughter who lived out of state to have sex with both of them. What unfolded were numerous women and underage girls in various states, a hidden life diametrically opposed to the image he had carefully constructed, until the house of cards collapsed.

For most of us who are dealing with less serious pathological *shadow* issues, exploring our role in denying our more unpleasant urges and projecting them on others will likely not be as dramatic, devastating, or catastrophic. The sooner we are willing to see how the *shadow* is working in our lives and to take responsibility for our role in this charade, the quicker we can begin to find the gifts in our *shadow* that will make us whole.

We hear the Carl Jung quote, "What we resist persists" so often that it has reached proverbial proportions. Most of us however do not understand that we are, in fact, **resisting**. We think we *"used to be like that"* and now we are *"completely changed."* That is why we say we hate that behavior so much in others or why we hate certain behaviors and the kinds of people who do them. We are blind to the fact that although we have relegated that part of ourselves to the shadows, it is still alive and everyone else still sees it.

When I am coaching people I usually can tell early into the coaching process what might be on their list of things that drives them crazy. When they share what is on their list, I ask if they feel they do any of those things. Most people like Katie are adamant that they hate these things and so why would they do them. The nature of the question is even foreign to them. Usually at that moment, I put the list aside until it might be easier for them to understand.

Frank said that at the top of his list was someone who was being *false*. He went on to explain how he really hated people who looked right in your face and were not being straight with you. Shortly after, we began discussing the reason for his coming for coaching, and it unfolded that he had been having a hard time in his marriage. Frank had a brief affair that his wife found out about because the woman with whom he had the affair knew his wife and told her. I asked, "Can we go back to your list for a minute and look at '*false*' again???" Slowly he began to recognize his own propensity to be *false*, not only in having the affair and then lying about it, but in numerous other situations in his life.

As we followed the thread of shame to the origins of being *false*, it arrived at his mother's suicide when Frank was 10 years old. The morning that she killed herself, she arrived at his school, saw him in the playground through the fence, smiled, waved at him and mouthed the words "I'm sorry," blew him a kiss, and drove off. She parked the car on a bridge some miles away and jumped to her death. Because Frank was so stunned and shamed by what he saw as the *false* behavior of his mother, he disconnected from his own propensity to be *false* until it was no longer visible to him.

As long as we continue to hide our shame and darkness, we will continue to be prisoners of our shame, and we will have no power or freedom to be all of who we are when we most need it. We can never fully appreciate our candor if we do not own our tendency to be false or our intelligence if we do not own our stupidity or our peace if we do not own our anger, and we can never fully embrace our kindness if we do not own our nastiness.

Becoming better acquainted with our *shadow* is a necessary part of continuing to grow, evolve and become successful leaders. In managing large groups of people and large projects, it is incredibly helpful to listen for the dissonance and duality from individuals as well as the group as a whole. Groups and organizations have *shadows* too.

We hear the voice of the group's *shadow* so regularly that it may not even sound strange. One example is the *them* versus *us* mentality demonstrated in the concept that *"they are out to take advantage of us if we let them,"* or *"they are totally incompetent and need to be managed if we expect to get anything of value from them."* The assumption that everyone is useless, stupid and/or incompetent without the brilliance of the company's team orchestrating everything is a sign that clearly demonstrates this dissonance.

As long as there is light, there will be darkness, so the reality of the *shadow* is not the difficulty. We all have *shadows*; it is only when we are blind to the existence of them that problems arise. The longer we persist in disowning our *shadows* the more frightening they become to us, the more we fear what scary things are hidden in there and the greater effort we put into hiding them. Deepak Chopra often says, "We can't fight darkness with darkness but we can switch on the light."

The key to unlocking our *shadow*—and the intense feelings of shame and rage behind it—is compassion, one of our *love*-based emotions. If we can feel compassion for ourselves for being so blind in not recognizing the duality we perpetuated for so many years, we can begin to feel compassion for the people around us who we perceive as exhibiting these very traits. Compassion helps us regain our wholeness.

Take a moment to reflect upon the two basic states of *Love* and *Fear.*

- How often do you catch yourself in a state of *fear*, and which *fear*-based emotions do you find yourself in most often?

- How does being in a place of *fear* affect you physically? What do you feel when you are having a meltdown?

- Have you ever observed yourself consciously make a shift from a *fear*-based emotion to a *love*-based emotion? How did you do it, and how can you do it more often?

- In your leadership role in your family, community or company, when have you seen your effectiveness diminish because you were coming from a place of *fear*?

- Identify someone or something in your life that has the ability to *press your buttons*. Look at the way you usually get sucked into the situation. Can you begin to see your role in how this unfolds?

- Make your list of five things that drive you crazy in others. What can you see about yourself when you look at this list?

Take a moment to disconnect from your surroundings and be totally present. Begin to practice the *Freeze-Frame®* process—

- Focus on the area around your heart, find and activate a joyous feeling or peak moment that makes you smile. Remember that it is not simply a mental image of this memory; it is the emotions of bliss associated with this memory and your deep feelings of heartfelt gratitude that will start this process moving. Inhale this blissful moment.

- Breathe deeply; inhaling through the heart and bringing the air low in the body, below the navel, as if filling a small balloon, to a count of 1 2 3 4 5 and exhale 6 7 8 9 10, feel the balloon deflate. Continue this exercise for a few minutes and practice this as often as you can throughout the day.

Remember that you are retraining your system to enter a state of calm, remain in that state of calm or return to it as quickly as possible when stressful events arise. This practice is a discipline. It keeps us centered and in shape mentally, physically and emotionally so we are truly present and prepared to experience the most important moments of our lives.

PART II

Our Life is Our Illusion

"You create your universe as you go along"

<small>WINSTON CHURCHILL</small>

Chapter Four

Exposing the Illusion

. . . and it is All an Illusion

I feel like I am the luckiest woman in the world. I wake up most mornings beside a man I love intensely, my soul mate, my perfect mirror who is always reflecting back to me who I am being and how I am doing (sometimes I do not find the reflection very flattering, and . . . it is always a perfect reflection!). If it is a sunny and wonderful day, or if it is not, I still usually feel like the luckiest woman in the world. I feel like the luckiest woman in the world because I come from a family that loves me, I live in a family that loves me, I am alive and I am living *my perfect life.*

I am free. Free to think what I wish, free to live, to laugh and to love how I desire. Free to be *whomever* I choose to be. I deeply appreciate how free I am in numerous ways all day long. Even though I am in a committed relationship, I have never felt more freedom in my life. I am safe because I am free and I am free because I am safe.

I feel I live in a beautiful place. To me, everywhere I look there is beauty. The hills, the plains, the vineyards and the cypress, as well as how the light hits those ever-changing landscapes, bring me profound joy. From inside my house through to what my views are to the outside, I recognize most days that this is the kind of beauty that brings me deep gratitude. I designed this house with beauty in mind, *my kind of beauty*. It was important for me to see beauty from every vantage point within and use every window as a picture to be framed.

You see, *beauty* and *freedom* are two of my most important values. Life without either would be torturous. What that has really translated to is a life filled with my definition of *freedom* and my kind of *beauty*. Someone else may not find such great beauty in any of the same things, and they may not see my life as free at all. The perception of others in this regard is not important to me. What is important is that I appreciate the life I created and that I continue to create a life about which feeling gratitude is easy. I know now so much more than ever before about how to create what I need to flourish.

Often when I am speaking about this topic, someone may say something like . . . *"sounds like you think you have the perfect life"* . . . in an almost snide way. I always smile and reply, *"Yes I do. **Perfect for me** at this time in my life . . . not perfect for you, not perfect for my sister, and maybe not even perfect for any of my friends. My life is only perfect for me. I live in appreciation that I am where I need to be right now, and that gratitude brings me more of where I need to be right now."*

When I began focusing on creating *my perfect life* in the early '90s, I had not the slightest idea of what it would be. Oh, I knew the characteristics of the person with whom I would like to share my life and the values that were important to me, but what *my perfect life* would look like was as big a mystery to me as to anyone. If you told me I would be living the life I am now living, I would not have believed you. It would not have fit my concept of where I thought I was going. I love big cities like New York and London. I am a culture person; I love museums, I love buildings and bustling streets, I love art, architecture, I love the excitement of big development projects, I love dining in fantastic restaurants, and living life in the fast lane. If I could stuff 35 hours into a 24-hour day and still get my 8 hours of sleep, I would be thrilled.

Who would have believed that almost 20 years later, I would be living in a small Italian town of 7000 people, an hour outside Venice, married to a medical doctor and waking up every morning not putting on a suit and not leaving for some urban office to finish the latest project on time and within budget. The life that turned out to be *perfect for me* could not have been further from my mind!

Luckily I did not color my requests to the universe with all kinds of stipulations . . . I just kept saying . . . **my perfect life is on its way** . . . **bring me my perfect life** . . . **bring it on now!** Fortunately, I applied my *Chinese-food concept* to attracting my perfect life. The essence of my *Chinese-food concept* goes something like this: If we are asked what kind of food we would like, and we say, *Chinese food please, oh I love Chinese food,* we will more than likely get a great Chinese dinner, we will be pleased—even though chances are we would not have expanded our culinary horizons much. However, if in response to the same question we answered, *Oh I love good food, what do you suggest?!* we might be introduced to the most amazing Cuban/Chilean fusion restaurant and not only would we have had a novel foodie experience, we would have learned something totally new. I have always felt that when we tell people exactly what we want, we may very well get it, and if we give people the chance, we may be taken on an adventure and given something we had no idea existed, and learned something fascinating in the process. My life has unfolded in a similar way.

My life is my **illusion**—whether I perceive it as perfect for me or not, and whether I like it or not. My life is always reflecting back to me exactly what I believe to be my truth, my beliefs about myself and others. The good, the bad and the ugly as well as the beautiful and free are all created here inside me. Then like a stage production, the actors and actresses in my theater arrive right on cue to play the role I have created for them to demonstrate to myself and others what I believe is true about me and about life. That is why I often jokingly say, using the most authentic game-show-host voice that I can muster: "OK . . . and what's in store for us today on *The Carla Picardi Show?!*"

How Does the Illusion Work?

We begin early in life to form an idea of who we think we are. This idea is further developed by others' views of us as well as their responses to us and our behaviors. Soon we construct a fairly solid idea of who we think we are, and we create experiences that further reinforce this idea. And then we begin to believe this is *true*. In actuality, it is simply the *Law of Attraction* in action—the attracting into our lives what we think, feel, and believe to be *true*. Then, as we see it reflected back to us by more outside reinforcement of it being *true*, we become more fixed in our belief that this must be *true*, and we create even more of these feelings. If we are creating positive experiences and receiving positive reinforcement, we may be enjoying the experience. If we are creating negative experiences and receiving negative reinforcement, we may not be enjoying our lives as much. Either way, it is all an **illusion** created and directed by us, arising from our feelings about everything, which stem from our value or self-worth.

It might be helpful to look at a small slice of how this works. Let us use the example of two men's feelings about foreigners living in their country. Man #1 feels that foreigners are a problem; foreigners take our jobs, use too much of our government-sponsored programs, commit crimes, cannot be trusted and are basically out to ruin our country and take away our freedoms. Man #2 feels the opposite. He believes that we are lucky to have a steady influx of foreigners, foreigners do the jobs that none of us want to do, foreigners are hard working, honest and reliable, foreigners pay their taxes and are willing to go the extra mile to make it in their new country, and they proudly respect the rules and customs of their new land.

Man #1 says that Man #2's theory is ridiculous. "I can prove that three friends and I have lost our jobs to foreigners. Our neighborhood has been robbed regularly and who has committed these crimes? Foreigners! They are dishonest and always up to something devious. My wife's purse was stolen in the mall the other day by a foreigner. Foreigners are out to ruin the balance of the egalitarian systems we have put in place. Foreigners are bad for the future of this country."

Man #2 says that Man #1's theory is totally untrue. "I have never met a foreigner like that. All the foreigners I know are so honest, compassionate and hardworking. My neighbor's mother had a wonderful foreign woman who stayed with her night and day until she passed away; my cousin had the same wonderful experience with a foreign caregiver. All the gardening in our neighborhood is done by foreign families and we won an award last month for the most beautiful street in our community. In fact the other day my wife left her purse in the ladies' room in the mall and a foreign woman came running after her to give it back to her."

Man #1 and Man #2 are equally fixed in their beliefs about foreigners. And, due to their beliefs about foreigners and their experiences with foreigners, both men continue to attract more of the same, and both believe beyond a shadow of a doubt that their truth is *true*. They may take it a step further and fight over their truth; they may kill each other over their truth, and maybe even start wars over their truth, believing all the while that the side they are fighting for is actually *true*. Both men are experiencing the *Law of Attraction* in action and have seen the result of attracting into their lives what they believe to be true. And both men's creation is an **illusion**.

We call into our lives exactly what we believe. We see evidence of that which we have been thinking and feeling over and over again, and then when it arrives we say, *"Look, I told you so!"* Life is simply reflecting back to us what we believe. Now if we multiply this by innumerable topics on which we have *beliefs*, including—most importantly—our beliefs about our own personal value, we come up with a complex **illusion**. Most of us find this difficult to decipher, never mind comprehend that we actually created, directed, produced and cast ourselves in the starring role in this *show*!

I realize how inconceivable it is to contemplate this concept of illusion and to see everything we have been taught to believe turned upside-down. It took me years to really comprehend the magnitude of this concept, and the more I am open to understanding it, the clearer it becomes. It is very complex to digest this all at once. It might be helpful to start by understanding how our most intimate feelings and thoughts about our own individual worthiness are being reflected back to us by the events of our lives. We see this reflection and we feel either worthy or unworthy—yet we do not understand that we started all of it in motion as a result of the degree to which we do or do not value ourselves.

If someone arrives on the scene in my life (character enter stage left) who is treating me without respect, I need to be conscious and immediately observe: *Where am I now? What have I been feeling lately? Where am I being disrespectful to another? Where am I not respecting myself and my needs?* This is often very difficult in the actual moment. It is much easier to be offended, to become indignant and to react disrespectfully, than to just notice what our *show* is bringing us now—however, this is where the real learning is.

Our lives are a perpetual demonstration of the level of worthiness we feel—reflecting it back to us via what we have created. We always know how we are doing if we could only learn to recognize the signs. If we could only remember to stop and observe—without judgment—all that is unfolding in our lives, we would be far more prepared to write a conscious, delicious, magnificent new script.

The degree to which we value ourselves at the deepest level drives the creation of our physical persona, the life experiences that unfold and the events of the world we inhabit. How we feel about our value in this moment is creating tomorrow's reality. Once we have the courage to acknowledge this, we begin to recognize that we might actually have a role in directing and producing this *show* after all. We only need to look closely at what is arriving in our lives, and what we have attracted into them up to this moment to fully understand where we have been in our past moments leading up to this creation.

Responsibility for Creating Our Lives

Taking responsibility for creating our lives in its most complete sense is a very foreign concept to most of us. Some may feel that this is blasphemous and we are presuming to be gods. I pose the question: *If it is all an illusion, why shouldn't we take responsibility for creating it and what prevents us from creating the most beautiful and wonderful illusion possible?* If we can choose how our *show* unfolds, why would we not choose the most magnificent story possible? If we are creating this illusion, why not write the script for kind, compassionate and loving characters and a leading man or woman (that's us!) that is full of self-esteem, living in perfect health and experiencing financial abundance? Wouldn't it be nice if our lead treated all the other characters with respect and love and was cared for in the same way by others? Is it not far more powerful to create our lives in this way than to complain that we are powerless, unlucky, a poor, unwitting victim who blames everyone who crosses our path?

Taking total responsibility for creating our lives is not about taking control—of ourselves, others, or even the situations in our lives. Often it involves learning *when* and *how* to **surrender** and **trust**! As Deepak Chopra says "Someone else flies the plane, but you get to your destination as a passenger even though you have no control of the cockpit." It is really helpful to remember that sometimes our role is simply to buy the ticket and get on the plane.

There are certain things that appear to be fixed, outside the sphere of our choices, things that we came into this life to work with, learn from, and are part of who we are—our birth parents and first families or even our height and the length of our legs, for example. The important factor now is *how we work with or against these elements and the perspective we take regarding them*. Taking total responsibility for creating our lives is about choosing firstly who we believe we are—starting with our value—our self-worth.

Ursula is a beautiful, successful, charismatic, dynamic and self-confident woman in control of her life—or so she thought until the day her life partner of 25 years walked out. He left no note; just a lifetime of clothing. Although he called her from the road to explain he had taken a few things in a suitcase and left, he gave her no opportunity to change his mind or contact him again. The fairytale life she had created was shattered and she was inconsolable. Yes, she had seen cracks in the illusion all along and she plowed on pretending that these imperfections were all part of the dance that couples do together.

After the initial shock, grief, and closet cleaning, Ursula decided that she was willing to start seriously exploring her role in what had unfolded. When we started our coaching relationship, Ursula was in overdrive—she wanted to get through this information, understand it and create a new life for herself as quickly as possible. She was "ready to move on." Although I realized there was an inherent impatience in this attitude, I admired her amazing tenacity and courage. In all my years of managing and coaching people, I have never seen anyone so dedicated to taking 100% responsibility for her role in what was still a raw and extremely painful experience, and so disciplined to do whatever it would take to create her perfect life.

After I explained the concept that *our life is our illusion*, I asked what she felt about her life thus far, and if it were true that she created it all, what parts of it might not make sense. She explained that her biggest frustration and disappointment was that she and her ex had never married. He had been married before and he had no intention of ever doing it again. No matter how much she would have liked to marry him, it was the one thing totally out of her control. In conjunction with this, he told her he did not want to introduce his children to her as it would be too hurtful for them. Although she never had any desire to have children, she realized as the years progressed that it was a loss not to have been integrated into this part of his life. The *gift* of not being married to him was that after he left there was no messy divorce—as she was the more affluent of the two. There was no awkward relationship that remained with the children. There was absolutely nothing left but the photos and the memories. She often felt that he died because one day he was there and the next he was gone.

We began to explore her most intimate feelings and thoughts about her worthiness and how these were being reflected back to her. It was difficult at first because on many levels Ursula feels very worthy. In this situation, the tender spot was in relation to the marriage issue. I asked, "What did his desire not to get married confirm about you that you believe is the *truth*?" Ursula immediately identified her story: She was "a player, one of the guys, not the kind of woman that men wanted to marry." Enter stage left the perfect man that would show her she was right, prove to her that the belief she had long held was, in fact, *true*. Ursula was tired of this story and she recognized immediately how she had written it a long time ago. She decided in that moment to write a new script.

Over the following months, Ursula bravely looked at every story she had unwittingly written into her script and systematically rewrote every line that no longer served her. She was committed to changing her life and fully understood the role of self-worth in the creation of that life. Today, with new script in hand, Ursula is preparing to meet her husband and living a life filled with abundance, joy and love.

Each of us gets to create the first thought, the first feeling that will start this process in motion. Why? Because it is our illusion, it is our *show*. If we believe we are worthless or have little value, our *show* will reflect that back to us by all the players in our lives treating us in ways that confirm our worthlessness. This reflection in turn makes us believe that we must be *worthless* and then—right on cue—more things arrive to substantiate this belief. We begin attracting more *worthless* situations that make us feel more *worthless* and the role of the victim is created. Where this newly-created victim goes with these feelings is dependent on the choices we make. Do we lash out in blame at others or do we withdraw into self-hatred and self-destruction? Either way, the downward spiral continues until we are ready to take responsibility—*able to respond*—by stepping in and becoming conscious of our role in this process. We have the power to change the whole show by changing our ideas about our self-worth.

"If you could put any value on yourself from 1-10, 1 being the lowest and 10 being highest, what value would you place on yourself?" Kersti Gløersen and Lennart Lööv of Allenergi ask this very question during many of their transformational seminars. Swedish teachers and healers, they are experts in many ancient traditions and demonstrate unconditional love in a manner unlike any other human beings I know. Since the moment we met, I recognized something in them that had been lost in the chaos of daily life. Kersti and Lennart have the ability to get to the essence of everything without comparison, and believe as I do that our core perception of our own value is that fundamental magnet that creates our world.

If this question were posed to you as it was to me, what would you say? Where would you look to find your value? Believe it or not, when most people are asked this question, we respond by deciding first how we feel about ourselves, and then assigning a number to our value. "Oh, I am not more than a 6" . . . "I feel low today. I am a 4" . . . "Pretty good. I am an 8" . . . "I would not want to seem too conceited, so I guess I will say 9." There is an almost embarrassed reluctance to own and claim our own **value**.

What in the world possesses us *not* to say "10"?! Why is it that so few of us are able to decide *first* the degree to which we choose to value ourselves, and *then* allow that value to dictate the quality of what we attract into our lives? Is it that we are comparing ourselves to Bo Derek in the famous 1979 movie "10" and feel intimidated because we do not measure up? This is not a beauty contest or even a competition for strength or virility; it is a centering of our self-worth—the *Law of Attraction* exemplified. It is like *not* voting for yourself to be class president even though you truly believe that you could do the best job. This is false humility.

If we could walk out the door every morning feeling a self-worth of 10, imagine what our day would be like. Picture how easy it would be to be magnanimous to everyone with whom we come in contact. People would smile at us because it feels so good to see someone who is feeling good from inside out. We would walk into our offices, participate in our meetings, drive our carpool and do our grocery shopping and everywhere we would go, our belief that we are a 10 would be conveyed to everyone we meet—and they, in turn, would treat us the way we treat ourselves, like a 10. After all, the people around us are simply reflecting back to us the worth that we have decided to give ourselves.

The alternative is to assign a lower number to ourselves, based how we feel or on the negative thoughts running through our heads, and life will continue to unfold as usual. We see a 6 walk through the door and we intuitively sense that this person does not care very much about their worth, so why should we? Then all kinds of behaviors unfold on both sides, which confirm that we value ourselves as a 6. It reminds me of that joke kids play on each other by sticking a piece of paper on another kid's back that says, "kick me." Until the child with the paper on his back realizes what has been done and removes the paper, kids will continue to come up and kick him.

Just as we decide ahead of time to be happy and then the things that make us happy arrive into our lives because we are attracting them, **we must decide our value in advance** and then we attract that level of value. If you find this difficult to believe, do it for a week. Decide you are a 10—that your self-worth is a 10. Pretend that you put a sticker on your forehead that says 10 and walk out the door. Keep reminding yourself throughout the day that you are a 10. Ask yourself—*what would a 10 do now?*—and do it. Smile at people as they go by, maybe even say hello. Give up your seat to another person if you take public transportation. Walk into your meeting and warmly recognize everyone—even the person you used to consider your adversary. You see, there would be no need for having enemies or resorting to a *fear*-based emotion; after all, you would be a 10!

Deciding to be a 10 would make us magnanimous. Our being a 10 would make it impossible for us to get upset about another's behavior because our feelings of total and highest value would reassure us immediately that another's rage or rudeness was not at all about us. We would understand that everyone is doing the best they can and we would take nothing personally. We would be generous and gracious because there would be no reason not to be! Does this sound like an ideal world? Maybe . . . and we each have a role in contributing to the collective consciousness every day by helping to raise our value instead of keeping our value low. Either way, as we affect our own lives, we affect the whole.

Once we can see that our feelings about ourselves are creating our lives and affecting the quality of life for everyone whose path we cross, we begin to see the magnitude of even the simplest of choices. If we are willing to see ourselves clearly and shift our perspective when it does not serve us or others, we will enthusiastically write a new script. In this moment we are choosing not only to create a richer day-to-day experience for ourselves, we are choosing to change our world.

Take a moment to thoroughly observe the illusion you have created for yourself up to this point . . .

- What do you see about your life? No judgment, simply observe your *show*.
- Do you like what you see? What is being reflected back to you that you feel is positive as you observe the events of your life?
- What are you having discomfort seeing as your creation—which scripts and scenes can you not believe you wrote?
- What characters, issues or situations do you now see as an illusion created by you? Can you begin to forgive yourself?

Make a commitment to do the ***centering of self-worth exercise*** for at least a week. Decide you are a 10—that your self-worth is a 10. Pretend that you put a sticker on your forehead that says 10 and walk out the door. Keep reminding yourself all day that you are a 10! Ask yourself in every conscious moment: *What would a 10 do now?* . . . and do it!

Use this opportunity to observe how easy or difficult it is for you to do this for yourself. What are you learning about how others respond to you as a 10? What changes in your behavior dramatically affect a change in the behaviors of those whose paths cross yours?

In this magnanimous mode of being a 10—write a new script for the life you desire!

CHAPTER FIVE

It's All About Perspective

Changing our Perspective

If we raise our eyebrows in disbelief when we hear Wayne W. Dyer suggest, *"If you change the way you look at things, the things you look at change,"* it is only because we have misinterpreted this statement as a cute little expression or slogan and we have failed to recognize its deeper meaning: **We are powerful observers and we are participating in the creation of everything in the universe and beyond simply by observing it.** If we subscribe to the idea that we create our lives, moment by moment, and to the concept that everything is an **illusion**, then we must acknowledge that whatever is physically present or absent, in this moment, is also an **illusion**.

The universe in which we live is filled with infinite possibilities, which means anything is possible. The mere act of focusing on something moves it from one of an infinite number of possibilities to a more *possible* possibility. Whether you call it magic or quantum physics, we now know that the act of simply observing something changes it, reorders it, and creates a connection between ourselves and it that was not previously present. When we demonstrate the *willingness* to see beyond the **illusion** that what we desire *is not yet here*—this act of observation begins holding a space for this possibility.

Simply focusing our conscious awareness on something transforms it into a possibility that begins to unfold. This is a very powerful concept. Taking this to the next step, when we hold a belief that something is possible—indicated by our courage to move forward toward our dream or vision—it becomes just that much more possible. The more we believe something is possible, the more it becomes possible, and with this realization we move beyond the confines that logic usually forces upon us.

To me, the following few lines from Patañjali, the Indian mystic who wrote the classic *Yoga Sutras* over 2000 years ago, describe exactly what I feel seems to happen when I begin a project in which I believe passionately and profoundly. I share this quote to offer insight into how powerful and inspiring a heartfelt vision can be.

> *"When you are inspired by some great purpose, some extraordinary project, all your thoughts break their bonds: Your mind transcends limitations, your consciousness expands in every direction, and you find yourself in a new, great, and wonderful world. Dormant forces, faculties and talents become alive, and you discover yourself to be a greater person by far than you ever dreamed yourself to be."**

I can see possibilities and opportunities in most situations. Even if something is not presently there, it does not put me off. Ingrained in me is the belief that almost anything is possible. I often say to clients: *"If you believe you can, you can! . . . and if you don't believe*

---

* The Mahābhāṣya by Patañjali as brought to us by Wayne W. Dyer in his book *Wisdom of the Ages* (Harper Collins New York 1998) p.17

it, you are correct, it is not possible for you." I recently came across a similar quote from almost 100 years ago by Henry Ford: *"Whether you think you can or you can't, either way you are right."* He and numerous other individuals have forwarded the understanding that what we focus our attention on changes our relationship to it, and then something indescribable unfolds.

I have what some people call a *can-do* mentality. I have made a career out of seeing possibilities where others say, *"It can't be done."* I love the expression *"It can't be done."* It is like a red flag waving in front of a bull; it sends me into action, and I silently reply . . . *No? Then watch this!* I love the magic of believing that something is possible before most people can see the possibility. I love the act of *holding the space* for what-I-know-will-be to arrive. I see it in my mind's eye, I inhale it, I live in it and I know in every cell of my body that it is on its way to completion.

Recently I was asked to speak on a panel in London about the process by which large urban redevelopment projects are created. When the woman organizing the seminar asked me for some details about my presentation, I said, "I would like to discuss the importance of *holding a space* for the possibility of a project becoming a reality." This, I explained, is a vital part of the initial visioning process and one that I was fairly sure no other panel members would be covering. There was a long silence on the other end of the phone, and then she asked, "What size space do you normally require?" I smiled and explained that it is an energetic space that I was referring to; it is *holding a space* for the possibility that this vision will come into existence.

The reaction of the seminar coordinator reminded me of the fact that holding an energetic space for the possibility of something we wish to become a reality is not exactly common practice. For many, the idea is completely foreign. Most people do not realize that an *intention*, set by a human being and sent forth into the universe, is a powerful force that actually creates. Whether it is a vision for a massive urban redevelopment or the launching of our desire to find a new job or our life partner, we are in large part clueless that we have a role in making the choices that create our lives and our world. It is hard to believe that even as we enter the second decade of the 21st century, this concept is not discussed in our families, taught in our schools and utilized in our work environments. Making matters worse is the fact that by the time we reach adulthood, most of us have lost our ability to dream, as well as our desire and curiosity to learn something new. Most of you reading this book have already decided whether any of this is possible for you. I intend to show you that it is.

Remembering How to Dream

I love dreaming about what is next in my life and feeling how happy it makes me to walk through these images of the life that I am creating in my mind's eye. I understand also how infrequently most of us take the time to really dream. Maybe we have lost hope, or are reluctant to get excited about something that we believe will never happen—because we are too old, too poor, too tired, too stupid, too ugly, too fat . . . Whatever our excuse, somewhere along the line, most of us decided that great things happen to other people, not to us.

As children, dreaming is something that comes easily. Provided we were brought up in a relatively safe environment, where our physical or emotional well-being was not threatened on a regular basis, dreaming is a natural part of childhood. We say things like . . . "When I grow up I am going to be a _____." We play house or hospital or dress-up. We create settings and situations where we play the role of the person we might one day like to be in a place we might one day like to live. This is natural, fun and fully authentic.

When we get to be teenagers, unless we have incredibly supportive and positive parents, we have already been programmed as to what is and is not possible for us. If we say we would like to be a doctor, someone may have already told us, "You are too squeamish to be a doctor." If we say we would like to be an engineer, someone may have already pointed out how our poor math skills would never make that possible. If we say we would like to be a painter or an historian, someone might have questioned how we thought we could make a living doing something with so little market value. Many times, we end up choosing careers not based on genuine desire, but based on what we think we can make a success of, and limited by the prejudice of our parents and other authority figures. Unless we are extraordinarily special or extremely stubborn, we have probably already traded in the passionate dreams of our hearts for something more *realistic*.

By the time most of us reach adulthood, we have not only forgotten how to dream, we are now squelching the dreams of our children with our fears and disappointments, all because we never learned that **it is through our dreams that we create the next moments in our lives**. Dr. Martin Luther King, Jr., famous, among other things, for his "*I Have a Dream . . .*" speech once said, "Take the first step in faith. You don't have to see the whole staircase, just take the first step." The first step is the dream. If you cannot dream it, you cannot create it.

When we write the script for the next act in our show, we are in essence dreaming. We are imagining what comes next and how we would like it to look. Most of us are picturing all the time how things could look in the future, except that worry and negativity cause us to envision a grim outcome. Yes, we may launch a dream out there and then we pull it back by thinking about how impossible that is. Then we launch it again, then we pull it back with a jolt—back and forth; no wonder so many of our dreams never get off the ground. With a small shift, we could just as easily hold steady, and create positive images about how things will unfold, and feel how great it will feel to watch it happen. Remember, it is all about perspective.

It takes courage to dream without judgment; to wonder aloud, "wouldn't it be nice if . . ." without needing to know "how" it will happen. The word but—when interjected into our dreams—grinds the creative process to a halt and stops our natural desire to dream. When we think more about the "but" and the "how" than we do about the joy we feel about our dreams, we are suffocating our creativity. Dreaming is nothing more than using our imagination to envision what is next in our lives without blocking the process with reasons why it is not realistic or logical. Albert Einstein once said, "Imagination is **everything**. It is the preview of life's coming attractions"

I often ask groups of students or conference participants to share a dream as if in a cocktail party setting. Each individual introduces him/herself to another, not by their name, but by their dream. After both participants have had a moment to share their dream, they find different partners and go again. It is important to get people in the habit of having several dreams circling around them at any one time. Allowing the dreams of others to stimulate our own dreaming process can be insightful. These dreams do not need to be earth-shattering; they can be as simple as, "I am taking a month off to travel around the Galapagos Islands" . . . "I am writing a book filled with the recipes and stories my grandmother shared with me about her childhood" . . . "I am learning to play the piano" . . . "I am teaching physics at Harvard University" . . . "I am a journalist for *The Economist*." Notice that even though the dream is still in its infant stage, how powerful it is to start with the words "**I am** . . ." These words are incredibly creative. Whatever we say after we say the words "I am," we are in the process of becoming. Developing proficiency for dreaming is important to creating joy in our present moment and fulfillment in all the moments to come. Henry David Thoreau understood the power of moving toward our dreams—

> *"If one advances confidently in the direction of his dreams, and endeavors to live the life which he has imagined, he will meet with a success unexpected in common hours. He will put some things behind, will pass an invisible boundary; new, universal, and more liberal laws will begin to establish themselves around and within him; or the old laws will be expanded and interpreted in his favor in a more liberal sense, and he will live with the license of a higher order of beings."* ★

When doing individual coaching sessions, I often bring up the idea of one's *future self* in a way that stimulates dreaming and feelings of fulfillment. I will ask the client to close their eyes and think about their life in 5 or 10 years and to breathe in every detail they can see and feel about that life. Then after a few minutes, with their eyes still closed, I ask them to pretend they are waking up in that life . . . where are you? . . . in a city, suburb, a rural area? . . . is anyone beside you? . . . what are you doing? . . . getting ready for work? . . . working outside the house? . . . putting on a suit? . . . getting in a car? . . . walking to your studio at the rear of your house? . . . what occupies your day? . . . what do you know about yourself in that life? . . . are you happy? . . . Tell me all you know and feel about your life," I prompt them. This whole process may seem a bit superficial, and I am always wonderfully surprised how much insight each of us already has about the direction we desire our lives to take.

★ Henry David Thoreau—*Walden* 1854 from the Conclusion

When we are in this flow, we seem to have all the answers to things we usually find problematic or frightening. From this position, we are heart-centered and we know how to proceed, what this situation calls for and what is right for us in this moment. Exercises like this actually change our present reality by altering parts of our nervous system and our brain connections. We see the possibilities in something that previously was outside the scope of our vision. It is notable that from this place of *future self,* we also are free from the voices of judgment and opinion that loop around inside our head, which prohibit us from seeing the situation clearly.

If we find it difficult to dream and to enter this *future-self* state, it is usually because our fears are so overpowering that they are blocking us. The ego has stepped in, clamped on, and is reluctant to give up control. The voices of fear and doubt that loop around in our heads and sabotage our dreams despise the very idea of change. If the unknown sends our ego into a state of panic, then it is easy to understand that the thought of a fulfilled, purposeful, joyful life would trigger the loudest alarm bells. If the voices we hear are filled with commentary about why our dreams are not possible for us, we know immediately that we are dealing with the ego and its need to be in control. It is important to remember that the ego is **not** who we are, nor does it dictate who we have the power to become. The ego is defined in Webster's dictionary as ". . . the mediator between the person and reality especially by functioning both in the perception of and adaptation to reality . . ." In this case, the ego is merely voicing its discomfort.

We must get into the habit of distinguishing this ego-based fear from discernment, and learn how to quiet these voices. It may be helpful for us to become familiar with our sabotaging voices: What are some of the situations in which these voices show up and what are some of the most common things they say? It is important to notice how often they show up when we begin to dream and just how disruptive they are to our creative process. Do not judge what is, just observe that these self-sabotaging behaviors are present, and shine light on them for what they are. If we continue to be stuck in one of these sabotaging loops circling around in our heads, we can use the *Freeze-Frame®* exercise to get back into our hearts. If the sabotaging voices continue to loop, then it is time to ask ourselves if we are really committed to feeling good and fulfilling our dreams.

In the past, I have actually dragged myself in front of a mirror, looked myself square in the eye and said to myself, *"Ok, stop it . . . this is really toxic and destructive . . . stop it now! I cannot stand to see you continue this self-sabotaging behavior, let it go."* It is important to remember that when these voices are in control, we have given away our power and we have lost our ability to choose. When I am coaching a client, I jokingly refer to this confusing and powerless feeling as *the inmates running the asylum.*

By focusing a light on this self-sabotaging banter and the destructive behavior that inevitably follows if we allow it to continue, it will gradually dissipate the frequency and persuasiveness of these voices. Ultimately, we arrive at a place where we can actually smile when we see our old saboteurs appear, knowing that whatever is unfolding in this moment must be right on track with our heart's desire if it was strong enough to evoke the voice of fear or self-doubt. This is all part of the journey of living a fulfilled life from the heart and making the kinds of choices that allow our dreams to become a reality.

Fulfillment is a State of Being

Imagination and dreams are the conduits that bring into our lives a deep sense of personal fulfillment. Just like deciding ahead of time to be happy, or deciding ahead of time that we are worthy, we must recognize what fulfillment means to us, see that fulfillment clearly in our mind's eye and feel it strongly in our hearts. Fulfillment is a state of being that exists apart from what we have—which are the results of feeling fulfilled. We experience fulfillment when we understand what values are most important to us and ensure that these values are being met.

We must begin by asking the question: *What would a fulfilled life look like?* Everyone has a different definition of being fulfilled and during our lives each of us may change the values on our fulfillment list several times. As we grow and evolve and enter different stages of our lives, some things that used to give us maximum fulfillment may no longer be as important and another value may take priority.

I remember as a young girl seeing a famous fashion photograph in some big picture magazine from the '50s—maybe *LOOK* or *LIFE*—of a beautiful woman in a tailored suit with a thin belt and imposing conical hat standing alone on the tarmac at the airport, with a prop plane in the background and two suitcases at her feet. I loved that photo and carried it with me in my mind's eye my whole life because it appealed to all my values: here was an independent, powerful and beautiful woman in control of her life, and free to travel the world . . . she was surely going places! I still smile and get goose bumps when I think of that photo because it represents a profound sense of fulfillment; what fulfillment means to me.

It is always helpful for us to periodically examine our values, for this is the only way we can assess whether our choices are bringing us closer to or further away from those values. Using the *future-self* exercise and looking at our dreams for our lives, we can begin to notice that our values* show themselves repeatedly. Our values represent who we are. When we are honoring them, we feel on track and fulfilled. When we are not honoring our values we know it because we feel frustrated and out of sorts. A good metaphor for understanding our values is that each one is a musical instrument in an orchestra. When we are honoring our values there is harmony in our life and when we are not, there is dissonance. It only takes one value—one instrument—to be off key, for us to feel the dissonance.

Values are intangible, ethereal and very personal, and therefore, there should be no judgment around them. No one, including ourselves, gets to decide that our value of *integrity* is worthy, our value of *power* is a bit frightening and our value of *fun* is pretty superficial. Our values are **ours** and we know they are important because if they are not being honored, we feel suffocated.

Our values just are—until the day we decide that value is no longer important—and then another value becomes more important and takes its place. We have already discussed my values of *freedom* and *beauty*, and moreover, within those values how I specifically define both *freedom* and *beauty* makes them even more personal. When I was younger, *adventure* and *power* where right up there after *freedom* and *beauty* as important values. Now *wisdom, peace* and *spirituality* are important values to me, and still not more important than *freedom* and *beauty*.

---

* Our *values* are different than our *value*. Our personal value relates to how we feel about ourselves, our self-worth, self-esteem, worthiness, importance and appreciation of all we feel we are at the core of our existence. Our *values* are not our morals or ethics, nor do they relate to society's definition of virtues. When we are discussing our *values* here, we mean each individual's feelings about what principles or standards are necessary in their own lives for them to feel fulfilled.

If *recognition, success, accomplishment, personal power,* and *fame* are your most important values, then my hope for you is that you are hard-driving and always in the limelight. What is important is for each of us to understand our values without needing to judge them. Then all we have to do is observe and listen for the music.

Take a moment to observe your perspective on a few **hot** topics
in your life that you believe to be fixed . . . for example: "my boss
hates me and I will never get promoted" or "I am not such a cool
guy and finding a girlfriend will never happen" or "things are
really bad in the economy and I will never find a job" . . .

- List the topics and describe what your *belief* or *truth* is
  about it.
- Pick yourself up and look at the same topic from a
  totally different vantage point 180° away.
- Do you see any glimpse of possibility that would
  allow you to hold steady in this new perspective?
- Re-frame the topic as a 10 might see it and hold your
  attention on this new possibility . . . for example: "my
  boss is under a lot of stress lately and I am sure if I am
  more supportive and compassionate, my promotion
  will arrive" or "I am a really smart and unique guy
  and I know that the perfect woman for me is on her
  way" or "in these interesting times there are so many
  new careers and opportunities that arise and I know
  that if there is one job out there it will be mine" . . .
  Hold this new thought every time your mind drifts
  to this hot topic.

While exploring these new concepts, notice any time you are
being hounded by toxic or sabotaging thoughts. What are some
of the situations in which these voices are showing up and what
are some of the most common things they say? If you are willing
just to observe that they are present and shine a light on them,
their hold on you will slowly give way.

~

Make a list of at least 10 dreams you know are floating around you now—your own personal bucket list. Remember to start with the powerful and creative words—"I am . . . ."

Breathe deeply as you look at your list of dreams and ask yourself—

- What would a fulfilled life look like to you?
- What do you know about your values at this time in your life?
- What values are showing up repeatedly?
- Which are your most important values? Prioritize them.
- How is your life in this moment honoring these values and where might you benefit from some adjustment?

PART III

Our Relationships are Our Mirror

"One of the clearest reflections we have to work with is the one provided by our relationships. Everyone we attract into our life is a mirror for us in certain ways. All of our relationships—our families, children, friends, co-workers, neighbors, pets, as well as our romantic partners—reflect certain parts of us. How we feel with someone is usually an indication of how we feel about the parts of us that they mirror."

SHAKTI GAWAIN

Chapter Six

Seeing Ourselves Clearly

Seeing Ourselves in Relation to Others

One paradox of life is that each of us must do our personal work within ourselves *alone*. We are the only ones who can conceive our dreams for the future and launch them into the ether. We are the only ones who can discern our values and choose to live in harmony with them. We ourselves must make the choices that will bring us closer, not further away from our dreams, and we *alone* have the power to shift to the perspective that offers us a more positive feeling. No one can do any of these things for us; we must do them *alone*. And yet, we never really know how we are doing with all this personal work until we see ourselves in relation to another. In fact without the reflection offered to us in the mirror of our intimate relationships, we can never truly see ourselves clearly.

Our romantic partners, our children, our families, our colleagues, our friends and even our enemies all reflect back to us who we really are being at any one time. The relationships that push our buttons most are the ones from which we have the most to learn about ourselves. These relationships hold the keys to what we still do not own about our behavior, and our role in creating and recreating both the joyful and the painful events in our lives. As we discussed, the more we resist seeing this reflection clearly as a clue to where our personal work lies, the less choice we have to use these moments to grow instead of suffer.

It is always convenient to think that—*someone is doing this to me*—for then we can absolve ourselves of any responsibility for what we have created. However, if we have understood anything about the **illusion** and our role in everything that exists in our *show*, then we must be responsible for what is being mirrored back to us in our relationships. The only person who does not see it is us.

When we find ourselves in a situation in which we are convinced that another is acting so badly that we absolutely must intervene, we are only demonstrating that some unresolved emotion has been triggered within us. When we judge someone's looks or actions as distasteful, we are not defining them, we are merely revealing that there is something inside of us with which we are still uncomfortable. When we feel the need to beep the horn and scream obscenities at some slow driver, we are only making it obvious that this person has activated some unresolved emotion within us. Everyone and everything along our journey is informing us and reflecting back to us who we are being. Our choice is to see it and make the necessary adjustments.

All relationships have huge value because they help us see ourselves—and our unresolved issues—so clearly. Anyone we consider "our enemy" or "against us" can offer us so much additional insight because we so vehemently separate ourselves from them. What is reflected in the mirror of our relationships holds the secrets to all of our emotional upheaval.

Of course as in all things, we have a choice. We can continue to resist the reflection that is being presented; we can pretend that it is not there, work to conceal its existence, blame others for its presence, or become the poor victims of this ugly circumstance. We can even get rid of the person holding the mirror. We can also choose to embrace the situation as a *gift* that has presented itself; an opportunity for us to see ourselves as we are in this particular moment. If we are still clinging to being right, we will be incapable of seeing our role in what is unfolding and we will continue the suffering for all involved.

If we have the courage to use every tense and awkward situation in our lives to learn something more about ourselves and if we make a concerted effort to observe what is unfolding in the mirror in front of us despite how uncomfortable it makes us, this work will move much more quickly. As our role in igniting these situations becomes unmistakably clear, we can begin to make different choices about who we are being in each moment. We can begin to put aside our violent or dramatic reactions and respond in a more sane and peaceful way.

No one says this is easy. The more intimate the relationship, the more difficult it is to step back to get perspective when our buttons are being pushed. If we are breathing deeply and have exercised our ability to remain calm for long enough to remember that whatever we are seeing is only a reflection of who we are being in this moment, we have a much better chance at succeeding. If we can slowly say the words . . . *this is about me . . . I am creating this now and I can just as easily choose to create something different . . . who do I want to be right now? . . .* we will feel an instant release of pressure, like the air is expelling from a balloon. In that moment we have the potential to see our role in our own pain.

Roberta moved to London from Rome 20 years ago with her new partner Marco, a successful banker who was transferring to a new job in the City of London. He was a "perfect" match and she was looking forward to building a life together. He was intelligent, sweet, kind and he adored Roberta. Somehow Roberta expected more intimacy from him than he was capable of giving. As the weeks progressed she began to feel her move to London with him did not bring her the fulfillment that he promised would be possible when they were away from the pressures of family and friends.

Roberta was happy to be away from their families too. Her father was an abusive screamer who berated her and especially her mother. Although her mother was an efficient and extremely competent woman, she tolerated her husband's behavior because in a sense she felt trapped by the relationship. Roberta's mother was a self-sacrificing woman who lived for her children and believed that peace at all costs was the highest value. Rather than confronting and interacting with him as an equal, she was just as afraid of her husband's rage as her children were.

The more frustrated and disappointed Roberta became in Marco's inability to be who she had hoped he would be, the more abusive she became toward him. She began to hate being with him as she hated who she was when she was with him. The more sweetness and understanding Marco tried to offer in hopes of restoring peace in their relationship, the more impatient and nasty she became.

Roberta recognized that she was angry and hated the fact that she was "forced into this corner of being my father." She decided to seek professional help, and discovered it was not easy to find a good therapist. The first Freudian psychiatrist she saw would not even look at her or speak to her directly. There were strict rules of how she must enter the room and sit facing the wall when she spoke. The therapist never asked a question, shared an insight, or said a word apart from, "I think we need to stop there." Her second therapist, a psychologist, was a bit more user-friendly, but still did not speak to her. The only words this therapist said that actually helped Roberta came after several months of weekly visits. "Therapy was meant for a person to grow and change." If Roberta wanted to continue paying to come, session after session, to complain about Marco, she was more than welcome, her therapist said—and, it was not going to get her anywhere. Roberta said those words felt like a punch in the stomach. By this time, however, even Roberta was tired of listening to herself complain. She got up from the session, her last one, and made her plan to leave Marco.

After Marco, she decided that serious relationships were too painful and that it was better to have superficial relationships with men who were incapable of committing to her. That suited her for many years until her own growth led her to conclude that it might be nice to have a more serious commitment.

It was only years later that Roberta realized that it was never about Marco. Marco was her mirror and she hated the reflection that was coming back to her. She deeply regretted that no one along her journey, not her therapists or her friends, had the insight or the courage to tell her this. When she began to explore her options for self-development, she decided to enter into a coaching relationship in the hope of understanding her role in the events of her life. For the first time, she finally saw how she had created it all; all the drama and all the misery.

Many people like Roberta go into therapy thinking that they will find answers for the pressing issues in their lives. They go to their therapists once a week for years and are never forced to examine their role in creating the events of their lives. No one holds them responsible for doing *their* personal work, no one compels them to explore how their choices have created and continue to create their lives. No one explains that the relationship about which they are complaining is simply a mirror reflecting back to them who they are being. Of course, there are a few wonderful exceptions to this. If you are one of those people who have been in therapy for years, this might be the perfect time to reflect on your progress. If you are still blaming your parents or your ex-husband or ex-wife or the girlfriend who left you 10 years ago or the boss who fired you, it might be time to re-evaluate your approach.

If you have been through numerous relationships or several jobs, and you complain about always getting stuck with the same type of partner or same type of boss, and no one is asking you to observe your pattern, it is time to rethink your therapy. If your therapist is not challenging you to see your role in creating the events of your life and how your behavior is being reflected back to you in your most intimate relationships, then your therapist is doing you a disservice. If your therapist is not pushing you out the door if you are not willing to recognize that your choices create your life, then it is time to ask yourself why you go to therapy. Is it a habit? Are you dependent on your therapist to confirm to you that it is acceptable to blame someone else or that you are justified in being a victim? No matter what the reason, you are paying a heavy price to hide and not live fully.

In any type of therapy or transformational coaching in the 21st century, your therapist or coach must be fiercely courageous and **willing to lose you for your sake** by saying just the thing you do not want to hear. They must be willing to hold the mirror up to reflect the very flaw you do not want to see. That revelation is the key to unlocking the wisdom you are desperately seeking.

It's Not About Being Perfect

I have known Goffredo, my husband, since 1998 and we have been married since 2000. When we met, I just knew that I would spend my life with him. We were not children; I was almost 43 and he was 56. He had been married before and I had been a serial dater—and we had both done our share of inner searching. Even with all the individual work each of us had done to prepare for this encounter, things were not, and still are not, *perfect* between us; wonderful, fun, exciting, challenging, beautiful, yes . . . and not *perfect*, because we are each other's mirror.

Seeing my imperfections is difficult at times for a *recovering perfectionist*. My father is a civil engineer, and his precision and attention to detail permeated our household where hard work and doing things the "right way" were celebrated. So, my belief, my *truth* became *"the more perfect I am, the more I will be loved."* Somehow it was easier to strive for perfection in my career and in my life in general. Those things felt more straightforward and easier to control. I knew that having expectations of finding a "perfect" partner and a "perfect" relationship were unrealistic and that was why I decided not to have any serious relationships for much of my life. When I met Goffredo, something shifted. I was more ready to look at my role in needing everything to be perfect. My father actually said to Goffredo, "We are really pleased you two found each other. I didn't think she'd ever get married. I figured they took the only man perfect enough for my daughter off the cross 2000 years ago and I knew that he was not coming back!"

Since I had waited so long to find my *"perfect"* relationship, I naturally wanted to make it the kind of union that one reads about in fairy tales. I wanted to be the perfect partner, to do all the right things, and I wanted him to be the same. Culturally, we are very different and yet very much the same. I am an Italian-American, and even though I am second-generation American, people in our neighborhood in the suburbs of Boston called us the *Italian* family. So, marrying an Italian and moving to Italy did not seem like such a big stretch. Goffredo and I both appreciate living in a beautiful, neatly organized, and clean home. We like the same foods, art, architecture, and share the same cultural roots. In addition to the subtleties of speaking different first languages, I knew early on that there were several cultural and even generational gaps where there existed huge potential for miscommunications. I knew this not only because we had already experienced this, but also because it was inevitable that they would continue to unfold.

When we met, I was living in London and Goffredo outside Venice. One of us would travel to the other every weekend. I would arrive on Friday evening to a clean bathroom and a new roll of toilet paper. Usually by Sunday morning I would ask Goffredo for another roll of toilet paper. Goffredo would look at me wide-eyed and say, "But I just put a fresh roll there on Friday," and I would say, "Yes, and it is Sunday. Could I please have another roll?" and he would say, "but I don't understand, how much toilet paper do you use, and what about the bidet?!" and I would say, "What is this, a cross-examination? Just give me another roll!" and he would say, "This must be an American thing!" and I would say, "JUST GIVE ME ANOTHER DAMN ROLL!" And off he would go to get me a new roll of toilet paper, mumbling all the while about wasteful Americans. This scenario happened more than several times. When we finally moved into our new house (with five bathrooms, I might add, all of which have an abundance of toilet paper!), our paper-goods supplier noticed that with all the American visitors we had, we bought more toilet paper than all of his clients. One day he said to Goffredo, "I wish all my clients would marry Americans!"

We can laugh about this . . . sometimes, and there are occasionally heated discussions about the philosophy of being wasteful. It is clear that I do not feel totally comfortable when my tendency to be wasteful is reflected back to me. That is why I cannot just laugh at the situation—it pushes some button inside of me. Goffredo runs after me turning off lights and turning down the heat even if I have only left a room for a minute. He was born in 1942 war-torn Italy and I, 13 years later in baby-boom America—no wonder we look at issues differently. On the other side of this mirror, Goffredo has not fully resolved his own propensity to be wasteful in areas that he prefers to think are not relevant. That is why he focuses on my wastefulness instead of his. He thinks nothing of burning the quantity of gasoline it takes to go from 0 to 100km/hr in seconds or to travel at 200km/hr on a highway journey. Although this dance is all a bit funny, it is a good example of how couples are perfect at mirroring each other's issues.

On other occasions, our mirroring moments relate to communication. Goffredo is a medical doctor with a deep classical education steeped in dead languages like Latin and Ancient Greek. He knows the roots of most of the English language and has **not** been timid about telling my friends that they are using an English word "incorrectly." He then launches into his explanation of the original meaning. We agree that he may be very right about the original meaning in Latin or in Greek—and now in the English language it has grown to mean something different. He finds it hard not to tell us, *"Well then, you are using it wrong!"* At these moments, I feel mortified and I usually say something like, *"Well, well, well aren't we lucky to be joined by Dr. DIDACTIC this evening?!"* as I fume and feel a rage growing inside me that shatters my perfect world. I feel humiliated by his pig-headed arrogance. This is when I need to remember the concept of unconditional love most and that he is only reflecting back to me my discomfort with my own arrogance and my own tendency to be precise and didactic in other situations. These circumstances would not bother me in the least if I fully owned my own discomfort around these issues.

One evening, when the last Pope was on his death bed, Goffredo walked into the room and said, "Well, the Pope is in *agonia*," and I said, "He hasn't spoken in weeks, how do you know?" Goffredo said, "He's in *agonia*, they know!" At this point, I was aggravated by his arrogance and said, "What, he rolled over and told you? How the hell does anyone know how he feels?" Goffredo answered, "Of course they know when he is in *agonia*!" I said, "HOW!!!???" and he said, "THEY ALWAYS KNOW!!" At this point I realized that Goffredo continued to say the word with the Italian pronunciation, which is not at all strange, and this provided enough of a hint that we were dealing with a communication issue. I stopped once again, retrieved the Italian/ English Dictionary and learned that in Italian "agonia" means the *throes of death* and in English "agony" means *extreme mental or physical pain*. We laughed easily with this situation as it was truly comical and we were wise enough to catch ourselves before it got out of hand.

I often use the word *fine* in that snippy sort of way. "That's *fine;*" "I'm *fine;*" "Everything will be *fine.*" I never thought I needed to define "*fine.*" One day, when Goffredo had done something that I did not really appreciate, I said, "Well, you went ahead and did it anyway," and he said, "You said it was *fine,*" and I said, "Yes and it was *fine,*" and he said, "So then, I don't get it?" I said, "*Fine* does not mean fantastic or great . . . it does not even mean *good* or *ok* . . . it means *acceptable.*" He looked at me in shock and said, "You mean all those times you said '*fine,*' *that* is what you meant?!"

I could recount thousands of stories that exemplify our mirroring each other. I have grown to understand that fairytale love, perfect love, is not necessarily *real love*. It is a façade where everyone puts on a pretty face and acts like everything is *fine*! I have learned to redefine perfect as *authentic*. A few summers back, I had a meltdown and decided to stop being the "perfect wife" and to stop doing anything that I did only to be the "perfect wife." Perfect is what is happening here and now, with all its imperfections, and through it all, I love this man in a way I never thought I could love another. I have learned so very much from our life together and I feel I am the luckiest woman in the world to have this chance to share this life with him and learn these things about myself. I know that until I can learn to love myself unconditionally, I will never be able to love another unconditionally . . . and I know that Goffredo is my mirror and until I can accept his imperfections, I will never accept my own. I am often reminded of the Jiddu Krishnamurti quote: *"Relationship is a mirror in which you can see yourself, not as you would wish to be, but as you are."*

The Courage to See Our Reflection

As we have discussed, all relationships are a mirror, and it takes tremendous courage to see our role in creating the image that is being reflected back to us. Sometimes we make every attempt to distance ourselves from that image, certain that it cannot possibly reflect who we are . . . and unfortunately—we are that too! This is especially pertinent when the person with whom we are relating is someone we dislike or consider an adversary. In fact, if we are truly honest, we learn far more about ourselves from the relationships that deeply challenge us than we do from the ones that flow smoothly.

Families provide a rich opportunity to examine these reflections. Most likely, we inherited from our parents the exact behaviors we hate about them and then we pretend we do not own these traits. Parents, in turn, find it exceptionally difficult to see their own unflattering traits reflected back to them by the people to whom they taught these behaviors—their children. So, the first and best place to look for clues to our resistance in seeing ourselves clearly is how much we protest that we are not like one or both of our parents. If we need to separate ourselves from and react to our parents in this way, then something we still do not own and are still not willing to see is being reflected back to us.

Children's reactions are shaped in large part by how they observed their parents deal with their own issues. If the parents are inclined to lash out in *blame*, then the children will learn this same method of managing situations where they are confronted with their reflection. If the parents are more likely to play the role of *victim* when their behavior is reflected back to them, then the children will learn this response. Most families have a combination of blamers and victims who impart both behaviors to the children simultaneously. In the rare situations where parents are conscious enough to take 100% responsibility (more often than not) for their role in the various events of daily life, children usually follow this lead as well and learn earlier than most to become more responsible for their role in everything.

It is possible to break this dysfunctional generational pattern through keen observation, patience and honesty. We make a choice in every moment if we wish to be conscious or not, if we desire to be happy or right, if we are willing to see our role in everything or not. In that moment we face a fork in the road; a choice point. We can begin to stop ourselves from resisting and bouncing into our learned response by breathing. We can recognize that what is unfolding in this moment is our reflection.

From this vantage point, we can identify these less-than-attractive qualities and acknowledge that we possess them too. Only after we have owned it can we begin to replace it with who we wish to be. In essence, these situations provide an opportunity for us to see who we are being, and this is a *gift*. If we can acknowledge those who provoke a reaction in us by recognizing their valuable function in our personal growth process, we are using the mirror to our greatest advantage.

Most of us however **never** make this connection between someone's actions toward us and our role in attracting and clinging to their behavior. Instead, we attempt to fix the situation. We will do everything we can to change *their* opinion of us, influence *their* behavior, and even endeavor to manipulate and control *them*. And it is never about *them* . . . we are simply resisting what is, and our resistance just contributes to the tornado of emotions and increases the speed of the downward spiral.

When a team member or client is in this resistance stage, I often use a simple hand exercise to demonstrate what is going on. I put my hand up in a *gimme-5* motion and ask them to do the same hand motion and start pushing against my hand. Then I say: *Do you notice how much resistance there is going on here? If you push harder, I push harder still . . . What if I stop and move my hand aside? What happens to your hand?* Of course, it falls flat.

Without resistance, everything falls flat. It is the resistance that causes and magnifies the turmoil. It is the resistance that creates the conflict. Without the resistance what we see in another is just a reflection coming back to us, a reflection that helps us see who we are being. When we are compelled to deny, negate or judge the reflection as *not me* . . . *"he did that, I didn't do anything"* . . . or when we get angry about the reflection . . . *"nobody does that to me"* . . . or when we revenge the reflection . . . *"I'll definitely get her for this"* . . . or if we choose to be offended and outraged about the reflection . . . *"how dare he do that, does he not know who I am?"* . . . or if we turn our rage inward and say . . . *"that always happens to me because nobody loves me, everybody hates me!"* All of these are just expressions of resistance.

We have the ability to choose the outcome of any potential conflict. We choose to be angry, we choose to be hurt or we choose to be offended. We could just as easily choose to laugh, to feel compassion or to do nothing at all. Our choices are only limited by the degree to which someone else's behavior triggers something unresolved in us. When that occurs, we resist the discomfort we feel rising in us and deny that it is ours. We point the finger at the other in blame for doing this to us, when all along it is just a reflection of ourselves. If we are triggered into anger, sadness, or even automatic obedience, these emotions show us that we still have more to learn about our reactions to this type of situation. If however someone's actions toward us or even around us do not penetrate our emotions, then we know this is not an issue with which we are struggling.

Many of my students tell me that they love my *Teflon Coated Raincoat* analogy and they think of it often when caught in sticky situations. When someone throws something at us and we are not prepared to see our role in what is being mirrored, it is like we are wearing a cloth coat that immediately absorbs everything, penetrates to our core and makes us feel instantly soaked, powerless and vulnerable. In a cloth coat, we are incapable of brushing it off. It has become part of us and we are feeling very uncomfortable. If we are at all prepared we may be wearing a GORE-TEX® coat that could be brushed off before too much damage is done, and this still takes some work on our part. If, however, we have observed ourselves and our most common reactions, we can really prepare ourselves by wearing our *Teflon*

Coated Raincoat. No matter what is slung our way, it will just slide off without us even noticing anything happened. Why? Because we are magnanimous and compassionate, we are a 10—and 10s always wear their *Teflon Coated Raincoats.*

We get to decide every day what preparations we make. We choose every moment in every interaction how we want to show up by how willing we are to prepare ourselves. We have discussed many methods of meditation, breathing and centering, all of which assist in preparing us to respond to a potential conflict. If someone is being nasty, rude, angry or controlling, and we let it slide—by not judging their behavior or taking it personally—we will soon realize that their actions are not about us at all.

Another person's actions are about how uncomfortable they are feeling with the reflection they are getting back about who they are being. In fact, in the face of their rage, our continuing to be calm, compassionate and forgiving with their insecurity may be further pushing their buttons. Our peace may be sending back to them a displeasing reflection about who they are being. We need to hold steady in our highest expression of ourselves and not alter our behavior to make another more comfortable with their unflattering reflection. We can send them love, compassion and hold a space for them to eventually see themselves as all that they have the ability to be. **It never serves us to be less in order to make another feel better**. It is important to remember that the more capable we become of holding steady in our authenticity and the more committed we are to being who we need to be, the more we may trigger people who are not.

There is a big joke in my family around the phrase: "he is doing the best he can" or "they are doing the best they can" or "she did the best she could." My mother is infuriated by the expression: *"Look Mom, I know you did the best you could."* She thinks that it sounds like, *"For a half-wit, you did the best you could!"* . . . I say, however, *"We are all doing the best we could have when the situation arose or else we would have done things differently."* Then the discussion ensues and my sister says, *"Lots of times people are not doing their best and they know it!"* and I say, *"That is true, because something is holding them back and because of that block, they are not capable of doing any better, therefore at that moment, they are doing the best they can."* Then the discussion goes into a place where my sister says, *"I suppose we should not push our kids to be better, force them to do their homework or practice sports or even encourage our employees to produce more,"* and I say, *"Why not, of course we can, and if they still do not do what we think is right then we must honor that something is blocking them from doing it and therefore, even if you do not think so, they are doing the best they can."* By this point the banter becomes almost funny and we all know what the other is going to say.

It is powerful for us to understand this concept that *"they are doing the best they can"* as it helps us feel compassion for another where there may have been previously only judgment and recrimination. It also would help the other person if we viewed them as capable and whole—instead of lacking in some vital characteristic. If we can see the person as *doing the best they can*, then we recognize that it is only the block that is preventing them from their success. When we focus on another as capable and whole with compassion and understanding, we are helping them by *holding a space* for who they have the potential to be once they remove this block, instead of labeling them as someone with a character flaw. We never help another if we see them as incomplete or lacking. Our role is to see everyone as creative, resourceful and whole. There is no guarantee that people will be able to get beyond their block in any particular situation, and our support may be just the vote of confidence they need.

We often hear the phrase that *"we are all things"* . . . and we have discussed earlier that we are the beautiful and the ugly, the sacred and the profane, the brilliant and the stupid. We are everything we love in others and everything we hate as well. Therefore, given the same set of circumstances, we could be capable of the same behaviors. Remember the old adage, *before you judge a man, walk a mile in his shoes.*

If we see people as how we would like them to be and we *hold a space* for that possibility, we are playing a vital role in assisting that person in being all they have the potential to be. Moreover, if we are able to hold steady within ourselves, we create the environment for another to fulfill our highest and most positive beliefs about them. This happens because people fulfill our *illusion* of what we believe they are and what we believe we deserve from them. We have a role in what we get back, positive or negative.

When people give us back whatever we believe we are going to get from them and it is negative, we may complain, *"I knew he would cheat on me"* . . . *"I was sure she was not up to the task"* . . . *"We knew that she would break the trust we placed in her"* . . . *"I knew he would lose the money I asked him to invest."* Our relationships are constantly revealing the role we are playing in creating the events before us, and we rarely see that we even had a role in the event, never mind what our role actually was. We have a role in bringing out the best or the worst in anyone who crosses our path.

When we encounter a disturbing or sad situation, such as a homeless person or someone terminally ill, it is doubly important to hold our heart-center, look them in the eye and let them know we see them . . . their wholeness and their divinity. Many times what stops us from doing this are the reflections of our own fears of poverty, hopelessness, or death, and we shudder away from these while at the same time getting sucked into their downward spiral of despondency. It is powerful to notice how these situations touch us. If we are capable of *holding a space* for these people to see their own pain without getting sucked into their emotional chaos, we would give them the gift of *a ray of hope* . . . and the secret is not to get disappointed or upset if they do not take or even notice our gift. Our wanting to change their suffering is about us, and our inability to tolerate their journey is our problem. We give ourselves the greatest gift by not allowing the reflection back to us to frighten us and by staying in a place of joy and hope throughout this observation process. By sending others love and picturing them as whole, we offer the most assistance to others in need.

If we allow someone to depend on us to a point where it affects our well-being, we have lost our balance and given away our power. Sometimes another's behavior slowly eats at our life until we realize that what is getting reflected back to us is our own dissatisfaction and rage. In the beginning, we claim that we are genuinely happy to help the other. Then slowly, their dependency becomes greater than we bargained for, or maybe we hoped that we would get back something in return for our efforts. We continue to help but now it is out of a sense of responsibility and obligation. Finally we reach a point where we feel suffocated and robbed, and we blame the other for "taking advantage of us," all the while we are the ones who allowed it. At any time during the build-up of this situation, we could have said . . . *this doesn't feel so good for me anymore* . . . and we did not. We did not have the courage to do what we needed to make ourselves feel whole. We were not being authentic, so what got reflected back to us was, naturally, another's lack of authenticity.

Monica recounted her story of how she was "*totally taken advantage of*" by a man with whom she worked and became emotionally involved, for whom she left her husband and child, and with whom she ultimately had another child. She explained that at first she was pleased to help him with his business; she enjoyed feeling needed and competent. She was thrilled to be treated with respect, admiration and affection. Finally someone appreciated her as her husband certainly did not. Mel made Monica feel beautiful and brilliant. Monica was happy to use her money to invest further in his business and to pick up the slack when other employees were unable.

When Monica got sexually involved with Mel, she was happy to have a place to escape her unhappy life and the responsibility of her child who she felt was more attached to her husband. When Monica moved in with Mel she was happy to pay for their new apartment because Mel was still financing his estranged wife and family. It was only months later when Monica started feeling *obligation* instead of joy from her role and she began to notice that Mel did not appreciate all that she was doing to contribute to his life. By the time Monica entered the stage of all-out resentment and rage, she had already divorced her husband and given birth to a son with Mel. This, however, was not enough incentive for Monica to take back control of her life . . . she remained with Mel for another 20+ years until he died and left nothing for her and their son. Since everything was in Mel's name and he was still legally married to his first wife, everything went to his original family, including Monica's investment in the business and the house.

As Monica described the situation further, she condemned him and used numerous statements loaded with blame and rancor: *"He captured me and deceived me!" "He enticed me into thinking he was someone different!" "He took advantage of me until it was too late!!"* When I asked Monica, *"why did you not leave at any time along the way when this was no longer fun?"* . . . Monica went deeper into victimhood and said the famous victim phrase: *"You don't understand . . ."* And went on and on in a state of rage and blame.

Monica is still very bitter and completely unable to see her role in creating this dependency, which totally threw her off balance. She is still blaming Mel for *capturing* her! Monica does not like the reflection that comes back to her when she observes this situation. She is fixed on being right, not being happy, and inevitably she continues to create more resentment toward Mel, even though he has been dead for five years. So, the only person still suffering from her resistance is Monica. Monica is not willing to see her role in anything. All she can see is that she was "too nice to him . . . too good to him." Until she is willing to admit to her lack of authenticity from the beginning, she will never totally understand her role in any of this. Most importantly, she will continue to be incapable of ever making different choices so that this type of betrayal does not happen again.

When we give away our power it is always by choice, even if it does not seem that way to us . . . and we are always one choice away from taking back our power. If we have lost our ability to use our power then taking it back seems futile. Until we see our role in creating and perpetuating our problems, we will blame others or become victims, all the while writing a script for the next chapter of our lives that we have no desire to live.

Our thoughts and our actions are energy and this energy creates the next act of our lives. We can either be part of the problem or part of the solution. At any moment we can make a choice as to how we wish to proceed. If we believe it is important to demonstrate a point—as Monica does by playing the role of the *hard-done-by* woman—we will continue to give our power away. It is more important for Monica to prove she is right . . . *Mel was a terrible guy and she was the poor left-with-nothing woman . . .* than take her power back, see her role in this situation, and finally move on.

It is sometimes very difficult for us to spend time with people who are stuck in a negative spin, like Monica. We all know people who constantly focus on everything negative about and around their lives. Every circumstance, personal or global, that touches their existence provides one more reason for their misery and further proof of how bad things are everywhere. No amount of our feeling bad for them or with them would ever help them feel better. In these situations we can help them more by holding steady, remaining heart-centered in a place of believing in them and seeing them whole—instead of worrying about them or judging them. We also must remember that no matter how we are related to them—parents, children, siblings, lovers—we are not responsible for their happiness. The only way we can help anyone who is in a negative spiral is to hold the mirror steady so they are given the possibility to see themselves and their role in their pain clearly. Then we can send them love and demonstrate it by living our lives in joy.

When we desire to be helpful to others in need we must clearly observe ourselves and our motives before we choose to enter into this delicate dynamic. If we feel an obligation to help them, or if we feel bad for them, or sad about their predicament in a way that leaves us feeling superior, we should be clear that our aid may not really help them in the long term. It may be helpful to first reflect on the old proverb, "Give a man a fish, and he'll eat for a day. Teach him how to fish and he'll eat forever." Although we may not be able to teach another anything we define as tangible, we can make an impact energetically by seeing their divinity and recognizing them as equal to us and whole. When we see them in this positive light, we are *holding a space* for them to see themselves in the same way. Sometimes these people are so fixed in their negativity, blame and in being a victim that they have lost all hope to see that they have a choice. Send them love and step back.

When some tragic world event takes place—either man-created, such as revolutions, bombs, mass-shootings, and war—or natural disasters, such as tsunamis, tornados, landslides, fires, or earthquakes—there is always a tendency to feel the heaviness of the collective consciousness and to feel personally sad or angry. In fact we are only feeling our own sadness or outrage reflected back to us. The situation has triggered feelings in us that are unresolved and we are sucked into the calamity, drama, and suffering. If we begin to focus on the details of these types of situations for any period of time, we will get pulled in even if we do not wish to get pulled in. No amount of our feeling sadness, anger or suffering can lessen the personal suffering of another or a group of people. The best things we can do to help are to remain heart-centered, continue to live in joy, picture the best outcome possible and send love.

Take a good look at the important relationships in your life . . .
just observe without judgment:

- How often do you find yourself dissatisfied with the
  behavior or performance of others? What do you
  recognize in this?
- What things would you define as recurring issues?
  What have you learned about your role in these?
- What are the chronic issues you see in your professional
  and personal relationships?
- Have you moved from job to job or relationship to
  relationship because you could not stand something
  about it any longer? What makes you leave these
  situations? Do you see anything about your role in
  these events?
- Have you ever left a professional or personal
  relationship because you could not stand who you
  had become in that position? Can you see now your
  role in creating it?
- When have you blamed another for your inability to
  do something or your doing something you did not
  want to do? What do you know about his now?
- Can you make the connection between a difficult
  situation in your life and your role in making it more
  painful than it needed to be?
- When you witness a sad situation how do you respond?
  Do you get sucked into the drama and downward
  spiral? Does it ignite your own fears of illness and
  loss?

Imagine you have been given an invisible Teflon Coated Raincoat. Picture yourself putting on this Teflon Coated Raincoat and walking confidently out into the world . . . living a rich and fulfilling existence.

Refer back to those chronic or recurring situations in your life.

- How will your new Teflon Coated Raincoat help you in these encounters?
- Observe your new self in each of these situations. What do you see sliding off of you? What have you decided to let go? How does this change the way you feel?

CHAPTER SEVEN

Being Who We Desire Others to Be

Finding the Love We Believe We Deserve

Years ago I remember listening to an audiotape of Marianne Williamson speaking to a group in one of her seminars about finding our partner in love relationships. She asked her participants to list the qualities they hoped the person of their dreams would posses. She encouraged everyone to make sure everything was there and gave people extra time to get their list right. Then when everyone was done she said something like: *Ok, take a good look at your list. Would that person want you?* (a gasp went through the room). *Until you become the person that **that** person would want, he/she will never show up . . . And when you do, nothing will keep that person from finding you!* That monologue left an impression on me because it deeply resonated with what I knew to be true.

We can only attract into our life someone who is energetically vibrating at the same frequency we are. To believe that anything different is possible would be like attempting to listen to a program on one radio station while being tuned to another station. I remind myself of this often when my husband does something that I think is so *not-me!* As much as I attempt to distance myself from his behavior, he is only reflecting back to me my own discomfort with the image I see, and my conviction that what I am seeing is *not-me.* The sooner I own the reflection and stop resisting it, the less suffering ensues for both of us.

People often think that finding *The One,* our life partner or soul mate, will solve everything. As beautiful as the relationship might be, all it solves is that we now have the perfect partner to help us see our reflection more clearly—and to evolve, or not. This special relationship starts a significant new act, and another main character arrives for the next big scene in our *show.* For me specifically, one of the most valuable benefits to sharing my life with another is who we both are becoming in this process. I feel very safe in this fiercely-reflective situation, and because I feel so protected and loved, I can look at many of my traits, reflected back to me from our interactions, and learn about my role in the dramas they create. I then can choose to change our relationship by choosing to change myself. This inevitably changes Goffredo. Goffredo changes my behavior by changing his and I change Goffredo by changing my behavior. There is no separate action, only a web of connection.

The way all of this plays out is fascinating. Goffredo says something I judge as judgmental and I get upset and flag it as judgmental. (I am obviously not wearing my Teflon Coated Raincoat!) This process unfolds with me judging him for being judgmental. If I can quickly recognize my own reflection and stop, everything will soften. If not, things escalate and nothing changes. You see, I find judgmental people difficult to swallow because I do not fully own my own propensity to be judgmental. If I can stop myself from judging Goffredo, I demonstrate compassion for both of us. I also stop him from the need to judge further. The moment he can see his own judgmental nature reflected back at him, the situation is diffused, and we are free of the dynamic.

Most of us never get to the place where we understand that we only change another by changing ourselves. We usually focus all our attention on changing the other and are frustrated by the resistance that unfolds as a result. We never really change anyone until we change ourselves. Since we are so deeply connected, we are constantly affecting and being affected by our partners. This is the dance of intimate relationship.

Everything that transpires in a relationship has significance; everything that happens is happening for a reason, and everything shared between two people is leading to a deeper relationship. When we recognize this, we experience a more profound life, individually and together. The most fascinating insight is the richness—the total and utter richness—that exists in connecting to another being, and learning to love as unconditionally as possible, first ourselves, and then our partner. This kind of relationship has the potential to be a *utopia* in the sense that everything is happening perfectly the way it needs to and the only problems that exist are the ones that we create for ourselves. If we can choose no drama and no stories, we have the potential to live in harmony and experience the peaceful and beautiful richness of love.

There is a commonly held fallacy that finding the right partner will make us feel whole. Unfortunately, if we are not whole when we meet someone, this is a guarantee that they will not be whole either, and this becomes a very different kind of relationship. Two halves only make one whole, not two wholes. The only way two whole people come together is as two whole people—a half and a whole person never make a match. So, if we are convinced that we are whole and our partner is not—we may need to take a closer look.

There was an oddly insightful cartoon book I read years back in a university human development class about the **C**s and the **O**s. **C**s always choose other **C**s to complete the circle and make themselves feel whole. Eventually both **C**s resent the other and begin to feel uncomfortable by being forced to be attached to the other **C** in order to create one whole. Since an **O** is whole and a **C** is not, a **C** attempting to attach himself to an **O** is uncomfortable and awkward for both parties. So, **O**s and **C**s do not get together for very long. An **O** however can choose to link with another **O** like intertwining rings, and each can choose to retain their own separate space or to come together when they choose. Still, both are whole—together or apart.

Like the **C**s and the **O**s, if we are not whole, we will find someone who is not whole either and then complain about how damaged they are and how unsatisfactory the relationship is for us. Sometimes we confuse being whole with the negative aspects of *self-sufficiency*. We single-mindedly move toward our goals, determined to direct every aspect of the relationship and stubbornly control everything for fear that our lives will not work out in our favor unless we do. We have always done everything for ourselves and we are incapable of asking for help as we are sure that we will be disappointed. When we are in this dark side of *self-sufficiency* we rarely recognize that we are missing out on our true wholeness. If we are capable of letting go of the intense control, we will see that real *self-sufficiency* is the ability to be true to ourselves, to trust and act in the moment. This is being whole.

If we desire to be in a relationship with someone that is creative, resourceful and whole, someone who lives a heart-centered, joyous, and compassionate life, we must become an energetic match to that; we must be all those things too. There are no magic tricks, and the mirror does not lie. Just look at your life now and the relationship you have, or do not have, and you will know exactly how you are doing, how complete your circle is, by observing how you feel about what you see.

The people who are attracted to us now are in our lives because they are vibrating energetically exactly where we are. Firstly we must own and not judge what we observe. As much as we might wish it were not true, we are attracting our partners because we are an energetic match. Until we are willing to take the first step and be the things we are searching for in others, we will not be capable of manifesting another person who possesses these qualities. Sometimes the relationship we are in surprises us and as we change, our partners become the people we desire. When we begin to shift to the place where we are *being* the kind of person we say we want, different types of people begin to show up in our lives. Again, these situations reflect back to us how we are doing.

Deepak Chopra often says, *"The way to fill your life with love is very simple; if you want more love give more love."* If you are being stingy with your love because you are saving it for *The One*, then you are missing the point. We must learn to be magnanimous with our love, kindness, wisdom, joy, laughter, peace, abundance, or whatever else we desire in a relationship with our partner. If you desire more happiness, be the happiness. If you want more peace, create more peace. If you desire more laughter, laugh more. The mate you attract will match whoever you are being vibrationally or energetically.

By embodying the traits we seek in another, we gain more clarity about the kind of person we are seeking. Then we need to write the script for the next scene of how our *show* will unfold. Describe in detail the character that will soon enter stage left. Who is this person? What does it feel like to be together? What personal characteristics are vitally important for us in a relationship? It is not helpful to say what we do **not** want; it is only helpful for us to understand what we do desire, articulate it, and then be it ourselves. Arielle Ford, in her book *The Soulmate Secret,* discusses that this "is the time to deeply and honestly consider your unique goals, desires, tastes and preferences. As you become clear about what is really important to you in every area of your life, you'll begin to send out a strong and consistent signal that will draw to you a partner who has values and goals that are similar to yours."

I recall becoming very clear about my preferences for the kind of man with whom I wished to share my life. I found it particularly effective to use the powerfully-creative phrase *I am. "I am sharing my life with a . . ."* and then described the kind of person he was, the way he would respond to certain situations and how he showed up in the world. This process of articulating what is important—no matter how foolish someone else might perceive it—is powerful, and it does work! I met my husband Goffredo months after describing on paper the person I wanted to attract into my life.

If we still do not have the relationship, the love, the friends and the things we desire in our lives, despite honestly feeling that we are living a heart-centered life and giving in abundance all the things we claim we desire, then we must look more deeply into ourselves. It may be that we are giving these things in hopes of getting them back **as a way to prove our own value.** This is different than giving these things with no attachment to the outcome. In this case we are *using* the process of attracting our soul mate as a *value indicator* because we do not yet feel our value. We are looking to an external barometer to measure our value.

We have given our power away and we allowed things outside of us to set the tone for our own self-worth instead of setting our own tone—instead of deciding ahead of time we are a 10—and, as a result, lack of self-worth is being reflected back to us.

Listening as a Way to See Our Reflection

Listening is one of the most productive skills that any human being can develop. It enhances every relationship in every part of our lives. It reflects back to us in every second if we are present or not, and how much attention we are really placing on each interaction. Our colleagues, employees, friends, spouses, and children always know if we are really present or not. They can feel it, they can see it, and they can hear it in the resonance or dissonance of our response. Moreover, our simple act of truly listening to another actually changes the stress levels in the hippocampus of *their* brain and calms them down. People are revealing in every moment intimate details about every element of their being and it is our choice whether to hold steady and remain present in this sharing or to disengage.

In our interactions, our values are revealed by what we are saying and what we are not saying; by where we are casting blame and what we are requesting behind that blame; through our sarcasm and laughter; with our body language and our enthusiasm; and in everything that is being observed and intuited by us. When we discuss our lives, and share our dreams and desires, we are exposing our deepest self.

If we can learn how to truly listen to others, we are not only fully and deeply connecting to the people around us and honoring who they are, we are demonstrating by our example how to listen. The greatest gift we can give ourselves is to learn how to listen differently . . . as if our life depends on it, because in a funny way it does. If we are truly listening, we are also accurately seeing our reflection and we are in a position to make choices about who we need to be for ourselves and the person with whom we are speaking.

There are three main levels of listening: *It's-All-About-Me Listening, Focused Listening* and *Global Listening.* The more time we spend observing ourselves listening, the easier it will be to determine at what level we are listening and to discipline ourselves to listen on a deeper level. Seeing my own propensity at times to be an *It's-All-About-Me* listener, I have worked very hard to develop tools to be a much better *Focused* and even *Global* listener. Understanding how we listen can be a huge source of insight, and not solely about more deeply understanding the person speaking. Truly listening provides a source of greater clarity about who we, the listener, are being at that moment.

In *It's-All-About-Me* listening, the focus is in the head of the listener, the running opinions, judgments and commentary occurring all while the speaker is speaking. It might be as simple as thinking, *"I wonder what is for dinner tonight?"* or other disconnected thoughts irrelevant to the conversation like, *"This cold weather is killing me . . . I wonder if I can get away for a week in the sun . . . Oh could I use some sun!"* all the while, someone is speaking, and can feel that we—who claim to be listening—have disconnected.

Another variation of *It's-All-About-Me* listening is when we focus on how what the speaker is saying will affect us, instead of truly hearing the speaker. In this case the speaker might describe a difficult illness with which she is coping and we begin to think, *"I hope this doesn't mean that I will have to pick up her kids from school this week too,"* or *"I guess this means that she will be expecting an extension on the project deadline?"* Thoughts like these indicate that we have disconnected from our potential to respond with any sincerity or compassion. We are demonstrating a level of selfishness that would shame most of us if we were able to see our reflection clearly.

Multi-tasking while we are supposedly listening is another form of the *It's-All-About-Me* level of listening that is not really listening at all. In fact, it is deeply disrespectful. Unfortunately, this is the way most of us listen most of the time. It is not kind, helpful, or even compassionate to listen to anyone in this way. There is an over-riding lack of awareness about the speaker's feelings and the impact that our lack of truly listening is having on the speaker. It is also reflecting back to us our incapacity to be present when we most need to be there for another. If we find ourselves complaining that no one listens to us, it may be time to stop and observe ourselves well. It may be we who are not listening and that fact is being reflected back to us.

Focused listening is where our attention is laser-focused on the speaker, on what they are saying and what they are not saying, on every word and every emotion behind the words. *Focused* or hard listening is what takes place when people fall in love and hang on every word uttered by the other, or when a mother is listening intensely to her baby. Every eye movement, nose twitch and sigh has meaning. The wise person uses this *Focused* listening to pick up all sorts of information about the other. In *Focused* listening we hear resonance or dissonance with the values a person holds and we begin to instinctively feel what type of interjection would be the most compassionate and profound for the other person in this moment. When we are listening in this way we know we are present because we feel it throughout our body.

As we begin to fine-tune our *Focused* listening skills, we will be surprised at how much information is available to us from what may seem on the surface to be a simple conversation. We begin to develop a new level of curiosity and become more adept at advancing the richness of every interaction by opening the space for more intimacy and understanding, while helping the other to feel safe and truly heard. Often when we are listening in this *Focused* way, others will ask if we are psychic, or have advanced intuitive powers . . . The answer is, no. We are just really listening.

Global listening is a more advanced form of *Focused* listening. Where *Focused* listening might be described as hard or laser, *Global* listening might be expressed as a soft focus on the person speaking. We become far more aware of everything that enters all our five senses. It is sometimes called listening on 360° because there is a consciousness of everything from every vantage point. It is also where everything that is happening in the world and even inside our bodies is contemplated as part of the total information available in that moment.

If we hear an alarm ringing while engaged in a conversation, we might inquire, *"Is there something alarming about this?"* . . . If we are getting a nervous stomach while listening, we might *ask,* *"What is making you nervous about this issue?"* In *Global* listening, the conversation becomes a dance where everything is available to help us understand what the other is feeling, and how we can best contribute to their seeing themselves clearly. We are holding the mirror steady and allowing the other person time to observe, while at the same time we are being who we need to be. All conversations may not require this level of *Global* listening, and knowing how to enter this level of intuition is a huge asset during the important conversations of our lives.

We can begin to see that our relationships hold a treasure of information about who we are being and what role we are playing in creating the experience of intimacy or the lack of true connection. The more courage we have to be vulnerable and go the extra mile to advance the quality of our relationships, the more richness will be reflected back to us. Remember that we always have a role in the enhancement of every relationship that crosses our path.

Naomi moved to a small village outside Manchester, England where her new husband lived. Steve was a lawyer with a successful practice and needed to stay local. It also happened to be where Steve's ex-wife Carol and their children lived. They also needed to be there because Carol owned a large car dealership and the children managed the business with her.

Naomi was very happy to move to this rural village as it gave her easy access to London when she needed to be there for work. She had no reason to anticipate that things would be anything less than civil and kind with all of Steve's family living nearby. She entered Steve's life long after his first marriage ended so she felt no part of the earlier drama. Not long after she arrived, however, she began to notice how people were compartmentalizing their social interactions with her and Steve. If the ex-wife was invited to something, they were not and vice versa. Naomi just chuckled at how strange people were about these things and let it go. She had plenty of friends who frequently came to visit from London, so the need to make new friends in this tiny village was not a priority.

When Steve's daughter was graduating from the London School of Economics it was decided that only her parents and her siblings would attend because of the limited entry. Luckily, on the day of the graduation, Naomi had to be in France for an assignment scheduled months in advance. When they later began planning for the graduation dinner party at a local restaurant, Carol decided that her siblings and their spouses, and Steve's siblings and their spouses should be there and she called to invite them. Both daughters' boyfriends and sons' girlfriends were also included, as well as 25 close friends of the graduate. The one catch was that Naomi was not invited. Carol said that Naomi was neither family, nor a longtime friend of most of the people coming so it would be better if she did not come. The fact that Naomi had been married to Steve for almost two years meant nothing. Steve was furious and threatened not to go to the party.

At first Naomi laughed at the petty ridiculousness of the whole event, and then later she felt deeply hurt that Carol needed to be like this. Naomi knew, however, that this was not the time to ruin Steve's daughter's celebration, and that Steve must go to this important family event. Naomi decided to leave town for a few days to visit friends in London so she could get far enough away from the situation to be impartial.

A few days after the graduation dinner, Steve called his daughter into his office and asked her if she had a problem with Naomi. She said, "No, I love her, she's great . . . no, really amazing, actually." Steve asked, "So, why then did you not think it was important to include her in your graduation celebration?" She said, "Because she is not family." Steve said, "You, your sister and your brothers all invited people who are not *family* and may I remind you that Naomi and I are married, so she is now part of *my* family." Steve's daughter began to cry, saying, "You know how difficult is to go against Mom when she gets something in her mind!"

Steve brought his daughter back to the house, and when she saw Naomi, she began to cry and apologize for being so insensitive to Naomi while explaining how difficult it is to be in the middle of "all of this." Naomi had been listening so carefully to everything that was said and *not said*, and at that moment she knew exactly what she needed to do and who she needed to be. She knew that there would be numerous family events in their future and she could not stand the prospect of this kind of drama, chaos and awkwardness unfolding each time. She felt deeply saddened that the children would be the ones to suffer the most because every important life event that should be filled with joy would be tainted with dread and apprehension about their parents' behavior.

Naomi decided she had three courses of action. She could give back to Carol the same rude and alienating treatment; she could treat her indifferently and see how things progressed; or she could bombard her with compassion, kindness and unconditional love. Intuitively, Naomi knew that the only way to really shift this situation was with unconditional love. If she really believed in the heart-centered personal work she had been doing for years, Naomi thought, this was the time to demonstrate its power in action and prove to herself and others that it really does work. Naomi knew enough not to take Carol's actions personally; she felt compassion for the woman—after all, Carol believed that she was going to spend her life with Steve as one happy family, and it did not turn out that way. Naomi knew that Carol was suffering and that suffering was being passed on to her children as well.

Naomi started simply by sending emotions of unconditional love to the ex-wife. Whenever anyone referenced Carol, she thought of her with total respect and love. Naomi had been holding Carol in her heart for months when the first big shift came. Steve was celebrating his 60th birthday and, unbeknownst to Steve, Naomi had invited some of his longtime friends over for a drink one Sunday afternoon. She also called the children and told them about the surprise. Naomi decided to reach out to Carol; she called and explained, "Most of the important people of his life will be stopping by and since you shared so many years together, I thought it important for you to be here too, if you would feel comfortable coming." Carol arrived at the party and said, "I just want you to know I came only for my children." Naomi responded, "For whatever reason you are here, we are so pleased." Naomi knew the courage it must have taken for Steve's ex-wife to enter their home and to put herself "on display" for all their old friends, and Naomi deeply appreciated her being there.

Several months later, Steve's sister was coming to Manchester on business and was staying with Steve and Naomi. Steve wanted to organize a lunch at home on the Sunday she arrived so his kids could see their aunt. Steve's sister said that she needed to save some time to go visit Carol as well later in the day. Steve's sister and his ex-wife were very close; both were only sisters within a household of lots of brothers and both had helped each other over the years as sisters would do for each other. Naomi realized how foolish it was to continue to play this game so she asked Steve to call Carol and invite her to lunch too. Carol accepted and Naomi reminded herself several times before the lunch to hold steady and stay in a place of love no matter what unfolded. It was obvious that although Carol was a bit on guard, she was truly appreciative to be included and everything went very peacefully.

The more love Naomi sent Carol energetically, the softer Carol became. Since those early years, there have been numerous family occasions and now everyone interacts like one big family. Naomi often says that Steve's ex-wife feels like an older sister who went off to university by the time she was old enough to know her; like they share the same family but do not know each other as two sisters would who were closer in age. At extended family gatherings, it has sometimes happened that someone who knows Carol from way back is introduced to Steve's wife Naomi with Carol standing right there. The person looks so uncomfortable and embarrassed, turning from first to second wife with a quizzical look. In those moments, Naomi usually says something to break the awkward space like, "Yes, Steve always travels with all his wives together!" and they all laugh heartily.

Naomi is a great example of how truly listening gives us numerous clues about what others are feeling, and **who we need to be** in response to create the highest possible outcome. Naomi not only knew who she needed to be, she continually made choices that brought her closer and closer to her goal: total harmony for all the family. This is a case where the reflection that was coming back to her from all directions told her she was on the right path. The more she lived from her heart and sent unconditional love, the more everyone found peace and belonging, including Naomi herself.

Take a moment to think about who and what you desire others to be. List not only the characteristics you are looking for in a soul mate, include also the qualities you look for in friends and colleagues. What might your list of requirements be? Some possible characteristics may include: honest, efficient, kind, compassionate, articulate, nice teeth, educated, clean fingernails, organized, flexible, good listener, attractive, athletic, polite, punctual . . . We all have different preferences—so do not judge—just write down what is important to you and be honest about your desires no matter how superficial they seem.

Looking over your list, notice:

- How do you feel about the qualities you have described?
- To what degree are you being the person you desire others to be? Where are you not an energetic match to those characteristics?
- Would people you know use these characteristics to describe you? What are the things people are most likely to say about who you are being? When you get straight *feedback*, what are you told?
- Think about a bit of brutally honest feedback you have received in the past and explore it as an opportunity to see yourself more clearly. What has an ex-spouse or former employee or boss said about your behavior? What are some of the things angry friends have said about you?

When we finally have the courage to see clearly and honestly *who we are being,* we can begin to make adjustments to become the kind of person who we desire others to be. Then and only then can we attract that kind of person into our lives.

~

Make a commitment to observe your existing listening skills and to expand your capacity to listen.

- How would you rate yourself, knowing what you know now about the different levels of listening?
- How would people describe you as a listener?
- Think back to a time when you were sharing something you felt was important and you knew that the person to whom you were speaking was not listening. How did that make you feel?
- Think of a time when you were listening on the *It's-All-About-Me* level. What response did you receive from the other person?
- Can you remember a time when you were truly present and listening on a more *Focused* level? What do you recall about the other person's response to your sensitivity and intuition? What prevents you from listening this way more often?
- Describe a time you can clearly remember when *Global* listening was required. How were you able to respond to the situation?

Listening to another is one of the greatest gifts we can give, and it is one of the most accurate mirrors we possess as well.

PART IV

Our Choices Create Our World

"Remember, we are all affecting the world every moment, whether we mean to or not. Our actions and states of mind matter, because we're so deeply interconnected with one another. Working on our own consciousness is the most important thing that we are doing at any moment, and being love is the supreme creative act"

RAM DASS

CHAPTER EIGHT

Are You Part of the Problem or Part of the Solution?

Be the Change

Mohandas Gandhi's famous words: *"Be the change that you want to see in the world"* have touched the hearts of many individuals on our planet. Yet it is difficult for most of us to see what these words really mean in our day-to-day lives and how we, as individuals, really can make the choices that create the world we want to see. Many of us feel that it is difficult enough keeping our lives from collapsing, never mind attempting to analyze our role in changing the world. For numerous people, what is going on in the lives of others is totally unrelated to their own struggles or successes for that matter. The majority of people do not understand that energetically we are all connected; we are all one.

In this beautifully woven textile of life, every action has a reaction. Movement in one corner of the fabric of our multi-textured universe means movement in the whole textile. This is the *Holographic* paradigm that scientists discuss. It is an indivisible whole, it is all connected, it is all the same and it is all one. And we, the individual threads of this textile, are also interconnected and all one. Nothing exists independently.

When we harm another we harm ourselves and when we help another, we help ourselves, both literally and figuratively. The trickiest part of this concept is discerning what *helps* and what *harms* another. Sometimes it is complicated to recognize that our own deepest fears are being triggered when we react to the suffering of others. Those honorable intentions of sprinting into action to do what *we think* would help another may be nothing more than a reaction to the discomfort of our own fears and may not help them at all.

I recently heard a story about a woman who was driving down the street with her 18-month-old child in the back seat when she saw a man repeatedly beating a woman on the street. Without thinking she stopped the car, jumped out and went running toward them yelling and screaming, "STOP! Stop that NOW!!" The large man stopped beating the woman and they both looked up at her, surprised. The beaten woman, her eye swollen and bleeding, touched the face of the man gently and said to the concerned woman, "Don't worry; everything is ok, he means well." With that, the fighting couple, whose ritual was interrupted, started walking away together. The concerned woman was stunned— then she remembered that she had left her child in the car alone and went running back to her world. She thought that she was helping the woman, and she realized in the end that she had no idea what was really happening in that couple's odd dynamic. She reacted to something in herself before she was able to consider and respond to what might have been the best choice for her and her child—and she was lucky that everything unfolded without incident.

Many of us would not have reacted by leaping out of the car and confronting the couple. We may have beeped the horn or called the police, or just said to ourselves, *"Oh my god, did I just see that?"* In most situations, we feel powerless and we think that there is little we can do to transform difficult circumstances besides sending money or giving up our precious time. Few of us think we can really do anything on our own that would qualify us to *be the change*. However, in an instant by being heart-centered, with the *intention* of changing a situation, we can send love to even the most horrific circumstances and make a difference—if we *believe* we can.

Admittedly, a lot of people see this concept of *sending love* of which I speak so frequently as useless and ineffective. We think we must charge forward and do something forceful. We think we have to take control of the situation, and show them the *right* way to handle this crisis . . . because of course, we know the *right* way. We automatically assume the other does not understand what is required. We may wish to consider whether this belief system still serves us or those we wish to help. And if the answer is no, we must have the courage to admit that charging forward may not be the best approach for creating sustainable change.

Many scientists understand that all of life exists in complex connection to everything—affecting and being affected by everything. In other words, *nothing exists independently, everything is connected*. This concept is radically different from the competitive separateness mentality that was instilled in most of us. If we are capable of pushing aside our old-fashioned, black and white, pre-20th century thinking, which has led to so much misunderstanding, suffering and destruction, we may be able to embrace this new paradigm of connectedness. An integral part of this new paradigm is making the choice not to judge what we *think* is best for another. If instead we can hold steady and send love, we will have accomplished the least intrusive and yet most powerful intervention possible.

Remember the old adage: *charity begins at home*? *Home* can mean our residence, our community or our country. It can also mean something as close as our spiritual home—our hearts. If we want to *be the change*, the change must start within our hearts by loving ourselves, and feeling our complete value and worthiness. In this state we naturally feel our connection to every other living thing. Although many of us find it hard to believe any of this makes a difference in the big picture of life—it does.

Our involvement as a conscious observer in any situation affects the infinite possibilities present in that situation. Our attention to any one of these possibilities participates in and facilitates the act of creation. This is the essence of the words: *be the change*. We can no longer deny that we have both a micro and macro role in everything that is happening within us and around us. From the function of the neurons around our hearts to the neuroplasticity of our brains, we are participating in what is unfolding in our bodies. To the same extent, we are also participating in the unfolding of a resolution when we send love to the most difficult situations. In the same way airplanes still take off and land, regardless of how well we understand what makes this happen, this new paradigm functions in our lives even if we do not understand exactly how it works. It is equally true, however, that greater consciousness, attention and acceptance accelerate our understanding of what it means to *be the change* and make us that much more effective.

We have already discussed how our perception of our own value is at the center of our creating the illusion of our lives—our *show*—and how virtually everything in our lives unfolds from this value. Our self-worth is the magnet that attracts into our lives all that we feel we deserve. Likewise, sending a heart-based emotion, like love, compassion, or forgiveness to a tragic situation becomes an energetic focal point around which the solution can organize. If we truly recognize and feel our value, then we would intuitively know that sending love to a sad, terrible or devastating situation is the most compassionate, least invasive thing we can do—always, anytime, anywhere and in any circumstance.

We have explored the concept that no amount of our feeling bad can take away another's sadness; it only contributes to more sadness. The same is true on a global level; no amount of feeling bad, angry, frustrated or sad about some tragic world event from the chair in front of our TV can contribute anything but more sadness and anger to the event. Tragic events never need more negative emotions sent their way; there are millions of unconscious people adding their negative emotions unwittingly. If we want to *be the change*, we need to consciously and deliberately send love and let go; then we can see how one small decision of our holding steady in our heart-center can instantly make a difference.

My husband is a man who believes strongly in justice; he is a crusader for the underdog and luckily the world is full of good causes for him to embrace. I have explained over and over this concept of not getting sucked into the tornado of events and contributing more hatred and anger, and he says he understands . . . *but* (the famous *but!*) . . . "But, what about opinions; don't people get to have opinions?" He, like many others, believes that it is important to *fight* for a good cause, and in the absence of an opinion, this becomes difficult. Of course we can have an opinion, and it is helpful to be clear that an opinion is only a *judgment*, an illusion for which we are willing to fight to justify. Does this feel like the most direct route to *being the change*?

When we first were living together, my husband would be incited by something he had heard on the news and come running into my bathroom reeking of righteousness, saying, "Do you know what *your* president did??!!!" First of all, my bathroom is the only place in our house that is totally mine. The only mistake I made was not to put a lock on the door to prohibit these intrusions. Secondly, I have never felt that any president was *my* president; he was the U.S. President and *he was doing the best he could.* Thirdly, I had already heard everything my husband was going to say in greater detail than the Italian news had presented it because I had just listened to the BBC World Service and National Public Radio—USA from satellite news.

"Calm down!" I would say. "Why are you letting this get you so upset? *It is what it is* . . . now let it go! . . . and please, close the door on your way out of my bathroom . . . thank you!" Then he would dive into a level of accusations and substantiations of the issue with a passion I felt should be reserved for an all-out nuclear holocaust or a monumental crisis of similar proportions. I would then ask if he truly believed that any of his ranting was helping the situation . . . or his blood pressure, for that matter. Only after much persuasion was I able to convince him to leave my bathroom and close the door . . . peace restored. Luckily that was years ago and he has since understood on many levels that sending love instead of opinions and judgment is far more powerful.

I do not claim that it is easy to hold steady in a heart-centered, loving place when innocent people are being killed and chaos reigns. And I also know that contributing my anger and hatred to a situation does nothing but further inflame the anger and hatred, something I definitely do not want to do. The only way I know to be who I need to be, to create what I wish to create, is to **be** what I wish to create; to **be** the change I wish to see. In this instance I must hold steady in a *love*-based emotion, sending compassion, forgiveness and love—not just to those who I define as the victims, but to everyone who played a role in the unfolding of that drama and everyone who continues to witness it. I understand this is a tall order. In the heat of the moment filled with shock, outrage and disgust, it is very difficult to inhale *love,* exhale *love* and send *love* without feeling the need to form an opinion or to judge.

I am reminded of an interview I heard in the early 1980s with the famous playwright Lillian Hellmann about one of her final books entitled *Maybe.* When they asked her about the title, she said that she had received substantial criticism throughout her career for what others perceived to be inaccuracies in her recounting the events of her life. In a somewhat off-handed way and in her deep, lifetime-of-cigarette-smoking voice she went on to say, *"Maybe* it happened that way and *maybe* it didn't." The moment after the event took place, she explained, there was no longer "truth"; it became her perception of the event versus another's perception of the event . . . and since she wrote the books, she added, her perspective is the one she got to tell. I often think about this little quip when I hear the recounting of some world event . . . *maybe it happened that way and maybe it didn't.* The fact is, we will most likely never know, so my advice is to send love and let it go.

I have been deeply involved in two of London's most controversial projects: Canary Wharf and the Gherkin. Both projects were written about extensively and in my estimation at least half of what the media reported was inaccurate. Since then, I lost my passion for the need to ensure accuracy in journalism—*it is what it is*—and no one says that *what it is,* is true. So, getting all riled up about the news seems futile to me. Not only does it affect all our bodily systems negatively and suppress our immune system for hours, it affects everyone around us. Most importantly, getting upset contributes to the collective consciousness of anger and hatred. If we really want to change the world, we need to *be the change.* And how we do this is by deciding in that split second to remain heart-centered; to focus our attention on our highest *intention* for the situation, and not get sidetracked in the drama or the false reporting of it. The alternative is to get sucked into the chaos and outrage, and in so doing contribute more anxiety, grief, and hatred to the situation. This is our choice . . . **to be part of the problem or part of the solution**.

It is sometimes difficult to distinguish what might truly help others from the things we do for others in an attempt to comfort ourselves. Before we leap into action, and go across the planet to build shelters, feed the hungry, and *fight* poverty, it would be powerful to first look into our own hearts and ask ourselves *what is going on here for me*? If we feel that we must recognize the suffering, lack of freedom and political oppression of others by helping them *fight* their cause, we must stop, breathe, and ask ourselves *what are my deepest intentions*? Perhaps all would be better served if we had the courage to hear the answers to these questions and *then* made the choice to take appropriate action. Helping people *fight against* poverty or oppression may seem like worthy causes, and we might serve these groups better if we flipped the energy of *fighting against* something to supporting them in creating what they deserve in their lives and in their communities.

"I was once asked why I don't participate in anti-war demonstrations," explained Mother Teresa. "I said that I will never do that, but as soon as you have a pro-peace rally, I'll be there." For those of us *doers* who actually take the step into action, it is important to be clear and totally honest with ourselves about the roots of our need to get involved in situations outside of ourselves. If we are reacting from a place of anger and outrage about "how these people are forced to live in such dire conditions" or the "tragedy of their political situations," we may be doing nothing more than adding to the collective consciousness of anger and hatred that already exists. It might serve us both as individuals and as nations to first ask ourselves—*What is prompting our need to intervene?* Are we helping because we are reaching out from a *love*-based emotion or a *fear*-based emotion? Is it our own fears we are attempting to quiet or are we moved by genuine compassion for their suffering? We will know if we are coming from our hearts by how we approach the cause. If we are there because we feel an outpouring of compassion, forgiveness and love for these people and a deep desire to honor them, their needs, and their culture, there will be no outrage and we will attract situations of love. If we choose to help the *fight*, we will create more resistance and ultimately get more *fight* in return.

In *Conversations with God*, Neale Donald Walsch says: "No one does anything inappropriate based on their model of the world." If we can remember this simple statement instead of ignoring it, we would be much wiser in all our human interactions. We may not agree with the ideals of certain people or the way they are going about upholding them—and remembering that most people believe their intentions are noble, even if we do not, could be a great source of information. If we spent more time working toward understanding another's view of the world before immediately judging it as wrong or bad, we might be more prepared to comprehend, if not defuse, *why* and *how* such crazy things happen in our families, in our schools, in our communities, in our countries and in our world. Look at any given family and you will see that not everyone views things through the same eyes. Translating this same potential for misunderstanding and conflict on a global scale can be catastrophic. This is where our listening skills and our willingness to observe our role in the things that are unfolding are vital. We may not be able to stop a suicide bomber from hurting himself and others, but we can send love instead of hatred, and compassion instead of judgment. We may not be able to stop an angry, delusional person from purchasing a gun and using it in the name of some perceived righteousness, but we can understand that this person, from his place of isolation, believed that what he was doing was justified. If we spent more time listening, really listening, to the dissonance, we might be better prepared to intervene sooner, and to act from compassion rather than vindication or rage.

What we each can do specifically is commit to becoming more conscious about each choice we make in our lives. We all know which behaviors feel good and which behaviors feel bad; being conscious simply means honoring this wisdom. If we believe deeply that something we are contemplating is good, right and wonderful because we *feel* and *believe* in its inherent value . . . then by all means we should do it. And if we are doing something because we are trying to alleviate an uncomfortable or *fear*-based emotion, such as anger, envy, jealousy or righteousness; or are involved in something we feel is tainted or inappropriate, then likewise, we should not do it. If we are lying to ourselves, we know it because we feel it. This is why it is best not to suffocate our feelings; our feelings are our compass. They help us to see ourselves and our choices clearly.

Sometimes we feel a need to *"protect"* the people around us from seeing themselves clearly because we believe *"they cannot handle it."* They are too volatile, too fragile, too depressed, too stubborn, too . . . something. What we are doing when we play this game is being inauthentic. We are mixing together several things, none of which serves anyone involved. Firstly, we have dubbed ourselves god, and we are deciding for ourselves who is strong enough to handle our truth, and who is not. Secondly, we have chosen not to hold the mirror for them to see themselves clearly. Thirdly, we deprive them of the opportunity to consider how we feel, and the chance to respond to our feelings—we just cut them off. Most importantly, when we stop the truth energy from passing between two people, we stop the love as well. In doing so, we have become part of the problem, not part of the solution.

In their *Allenergi* Seminars, Kersti Gløersen and Lennart Lööv often discuss this concept by using the analogy of a tennis match. Our feelings are our truth, our authenticity, and when we decide not to share with another how we are feeling about something that concerns both parties, we stop being authentic. It is as if we are holding the ball instead of sending it back and the game comes to a halt. The other person always knows we are holding the ball and have stopped the play, even if they do not know what caused us to stop. There is a lie circling and the person who stopped the ball in play has also stopped relating, and in so doing has stopped the flow of love. Sometimes we even lie to ourselves by saying that we did it because we did not think that the other person could handle our truth. What we are really saying is that we did not have the courage to share our truth and the resultant shot back to us. When we do not give the other person an opportunity to respond, we are robbing the relationship of the possibility of continuing to evolve. The ball was in our court and then we stopped the action. When on the other hand we have the courage to fire the ball back, no matter how difficult it seems in the moment, we are respecting the other with our honesty and authenticity, also known as our love. When we have the courage to be authentic, the ball moves to the other's court and now the other person is responsible for keeping the game going. If we could see this dance clearly for what it is, we would never allow ourselves to be left holding the ball.

Jonathan came from a wealthy and famous family. His father and mother split up when he was very young. Initially, he spent summers in the English countryside with his father and returned to America in autumn to live with his mother and start attending school. Whenever his mother met another man, Jonathan would be sent back to live with his father and as soon as the relationship would end, she would demand him back. Each man she met would bring her to a different place: California, Texas, New York or Connecticut, and there she would remain after the relationship ended. Jonathan would be dragged back into her life like an object to start another new school and to create another new life. He had always felt his mother was selfish and irresponsible; more significantly he felt that he himself was unloved and irrelevant.

As Jonathan got older he wanted desperately to tell his mother how he felt but since he was brought up in an old-fashioned household where a child never talks back to his parent, he could not bring himself around to tell her. As time passed, it was easier to avoid her altogether as he knew if he spent too much time with her he would probably blurt out something deeply sarcastic and disrespectful. Eventually she died without him ever having a truthful conversation with her about how he felt. Jonathan was genuinely depressed and at the same time enraged with himself because of his incapacity to communicate his feelings of being unloved and irrelevant.

Jonathan had stopped the flow of love decades earlier and it was only after his mother's death that he realized what he had done. He held the ball and stopped the game, without ever giving his mother a chance to send the ball back into his court. He never gave her a chance to share her true feelings either. Jonathan had a different excuse every decade. At first he said that he was afraid he would kill her with his rage, then, after almost two decades of therapy, he said that he had resolved it enough within himself and he did not need to bring her into it. Then after another decade he realized he was still angry at her and by that point he decided that she was too fragile to deal with a confrontational and emotional conversation.

Ultimately, Jonathan stopped his own capacity to love when he made the choice to stop communicating with his mother about anything of substance. He also never got a chance to see if she was willing to play the game—because he stopped the game before it ever began. He may have seen a whole new side of his mother. He may have learned how much she truly loved him and how deeply sorry she was for putting her men before him or how much she thought he hated her for what she had done—which prompted her to keep her distance from him. He might have given both of them an opportunity to heal their relationship and to forge a new connection based on honesty, trust and authenticity.

Although Jonathan cannot change the past, he can use this experience to make different choices in his life. He can now have the conversation with his mother in his heart and say the things he had always wanted to say and he might be able to let go of some conflict he still holds. He can also use this as an occasion to be authentic with any outstanding relationships where he is withholding his love by stopping the flow of communication. His mother's death caused Jonathan to realize that whenever he has felt frightened to say what he sincerely felt, he would play the game of *I'm taking my ball and going home*. He had never noticed until recently his role in stopping the flow of love, and how this had affected so many of his relationships. Lately, he has been more conscious about being more authentic; opening up long ago closed dialogues and tossing a few of those balls left in his court decades ago back into the other person's court.

Jonathan is not much different than most of us. We all have balls sitting in our court. Something happens that stops us from authentically communicating. We become afraid to toss the ball back for all kinds of reasons that our fears justify until we are convinced it is the absolute *truth*. Some design their whole lives around this "truth," when in essence it is only our illusion of what transpired. The only thing real is that we stopped the game with the ball in our court—and at any time we can change that by picking up the ball and tossing it back over the net. We need only to open our hearts to our vulnerability and shame, and share our authentic feelings to get the ball rolling and the love flowing again. Of course, there are no guarantees that after so long the person on the other side of the court will still be willing to play, and that is not important. The important issue is that we have the courage to get things going again, to *be the change.*

The Buck Stops Here

My father often used the expression *the buck stops here* while pointing at one or all of us kids as a means of making it clear that he was holding us responsible for something. This was an expression popular in my father's time because Harry S. Truman, U.S. President from 1945-1953, kept a sign with that phrase on his desk in the Oval Office. It is said to have originated from the game of poker in the "Wild West" where a knife with a buckhorn handle was used to indicate the person whose turn it was to deal by placing it in front of him as a marker. If the player did not wish to deal, he could pass the "buck" to the next player. This is the kind of expression that is almost impossible to translate with any meaning into another language, and *the buck stops here* is the first expression I think of when discussing the idea of taking 100% responsibility for our lives.

The fact is, *the buck does stop here,* right in front of each and every one of us, and at any moment we can choose to step up, take responsibility, and create our lives exactly as we desire them to be—and we can also choose to pass the buck. Along with making the choice to see and feel our own value, this is one of the most important choices we will ever make. Every concept we have explored on these pages represents a significant step in helping us understand the importance of *the buck stops here* and what each of us needs to do, and who each of us needs to be, to make the choices required to continue taking responsibility for our lives day after day. We must be vigilantly conscious—making the choices that will keep us connected to source energy and keep us in harmony with our higher self and our deepest desires.

Many people think that always being conscious of being conscious takes too much work. In fact to most people, the whole concept of consciousness is a bit overwhelming. The other evening at dinner with a group of friends, we were discussing this topic. One woman said, *"Are you really saying that I am supposed to think about everything I say and do in this light? That would be so tedious and exhausting!"* "Yes," I said, "and incredibly powerful! Welcome to the world of consciousness." For someone like my friend who loves to control everyone and everything around her, and is deeply frustrated by the things she is not able to control, here is something she can actually control: *her choice to observe her role in her moment-to-moment thoughts, words and actions, and summon the courage to make different choices that will make change possible in her controlled life.*

We are responsible for our lives either way, so is it not more powerful to understand what is going on and to use the system to our advantage? The alternative is to spend our lives cleaning up the mess of our unconsciousness while pretending we were poor victims who had no idea what was happening to us; and in the process never really appreciating or taking full advantage of the opportunity to live our lives to their fullest.

Many people say that living at this level of consciousness takes away all the fun! This mindset translates into other areas as well . . . *"I would rather take a blood-pressure pill than watch what I eat and lose weight"* or *"I always get heartburn after I eat but I just take a pill for reflux because I have no intention of changing my diet"* or *"I know I am borderline diabetic but I adore bread and sugar!"* or *"I am so tired of everyone telling me to get some exercise—it is so boring to workout!"* or *"I know that breathing and meditation would help my anxiety but I just don't have time and this little pill does the trick."* Many of us are simply unwilling to take responsibility for our lives if we have to make different choices in order to achieve it. For many, it is easier to give our power away and complain about our situation than to have the courage to make different life choices. Most of us realize too late—and only if we are willing to be totally honest with ourselves—that we could have prevented much of our suffering by making different choices. If we truly understood what our feelings of value and worthiness were attracting, we may have seen sooner the ways in which we were sabotaging our lives.

Sometimes people say that living at this level of consciousness sounds interesting but . . . *"I have a family to take care of and this is a very selfish way to live."* Perhaps we have forgotten that if we do not honor ourselves we will not be able to help anyone else. Taking care of ourselves first is our duty, not a luxury. When we are on an airplane and the flight attendants are explaining the procedure around the use of oxygen masks, no one says that only the selfish mother puts on her mask first. In fact they are very clear that first we must put on our mask and then help others needing our assistance. Why? Because if we do not get what we need and become incapacitated, who will help our child, or any other person needing assistance? It is our responsibility to help ourselves so we are prepared to perform our duty when the opportunity arises to be of service.

Years ago I heard a mother talking about filling the love cups of all of her family. She described how at first she thought of herself as the source and would keep filling everyone's glasses, even if there was practically nothing left in her own pitcher. Then one day she woke up to the fact that if she did not do everything required to keep her pitcher full, no one would ever get a sufficient amount because she would always be serving up love in limited quantities. She decided then that the most important thing she could do for her family was to do something restorative for herself every day, for only this would ensure that her abundant source of love would continue to be available. This allowed her to be magnanimous instead of resentful when someone asked for more.

Lucy is a young mother about to turn 40 years old. She has a husband and two children, ages five and eight, and she always felt stretched to the point of suffocation. She came to our coaching relationship in a fragile state and it soon became apparent that she might just be capable of packing a few things in a bag, leaving everything behind and never looking back.

Lucy was not a woman who made choices about anything in her life. She met her husband, and after a few passionate months together she found herself pregnant. They got married and a few years later another unplanned child arrived. Lucy's life was one big stressful experience in which she felt everything was just happening to her and she had no control. She was working harder at her career than ever and enjoying it less. Her boss was expecting more and more from her and she felt she had little choice in setting boundaries. Her husband's business was not doing so well and she felt she did not have the luxury of quitting. She was feeling bitter, angry and totally trapped in her life.

Lucy started to go out with friends at night for some fun and found she was feeling guilty for leaving her husband and kids. Because of this guilt she did not even enjoy herself on these regular outings. Her friends often experienced her as moody and commented on how much of their time together she spent complaining about her life. When she was home doing things with the family she resented the fact that she was not free to be doing what she wished. This dance of not being present in any place of her life had been going on for long enough that she was exhausted and felt that she had nothing more to give. There was a part of her secretly wishing her husband would leave her so at least she would be free of one obligation.

Lucy came from a family where her mother dedicated her whole life to being the perfect wife and mother. That was her mother's only role and all she ever wanted to do. Lucy hated that role model and at the same time, she felt guilty for not making a similar sacrifice. When Lucy looked at the *choice-less* choices of her life, one after the other, she began to see her role in creating her misery and how she almost relished sharing the next victim story to prove how little control she had in her own existence. She realized that she had a choice in that very moment, a choice to make her first real and conscious choice. Lucy could throw everything away and run from her "terrible" life—something she both feared doing and fantasized about having the courage to do—or she could finally acknowledge how she created all of this by not taking responsibility for her needs. Ultimately, realizing that she loved her husband and kids and did not want to destroy everything they had built, she chose the latter.

She began taking responsibility for being whole and feeling her best so she could be all she needed to be for herself first, and then for the others that depended on her. She stopped working her crazy hours and told her boss that she had made a personal choice to cut back to a 30-hour week. She began working out again, meditating and practicing yoga. She started noticing when she was not present in whatever she was doing and pulled herself back to the moment to enjoy fully what was happening *now*. Her friends were the first to recognize how she seemed to be following the details of their stories, participating in the conversations and even laughing with them. Her husband was so happy to see her joining in conversation with him instead of her previous yes/no responses, and contributing to the parenting of the children with joy rather than obligation. Even her kids asked her if she was "happy now." Lucy saw how close she came to sabotaging her life by forgetting that she was the one responsible for taking care of herself and making sure that her pitcher was full every day, day after day. There was no one she could blame for this oversight; the suffering she experienced she imposed upon herself, even if she did not realize she was doing it at the time. Lucy finally understood that only she was responsible for making the choices that ensured she would live in joy and fulfillment, and she was now ready to embrace her new life.

The most powerful opportunity we have to *be the change*—both individually and globally—is to recognize our role in everything happening in every moment. We are always either **part of the problem** or **part of the solution**. If we can remember to notice and ask ourselves this question in every conscious moment . . . *"right now am I being part of the problem or part of the solution?"* . . . we would create an opportunity for something new and different to happen and we would bring ourselves that much closer to a shift. The moment we recognize that we are *part of the problem*, having the courage to surrender and let go of the limiting behavior is our best option. It means we have seen our role, adjusted our behavior and stepped into being the change.

Take a moment to observe events in your life where you might be *part of the problem*. What do you see about your response now that may not have been part of your understanding before?

- When have you not taken responsibility for your own happiness—for filling your own pitcher—and what were the consequences?

- What is your role in your health issues? How have you responded to recommendations for your health (for example, to lose weight, cut sugars, reduce salt, change your diet, get more exercise, stop smoking or drinking)? How can you shift into being *part of the solution*?

- What behaviors do you most commonly demonstrate in dealing with tragic events? Are you an angry table beater? Do you rant and rave about how "people should be . . . ."? Do you become despondent and incapable of shaking off the horrific nature of the event? Do you bring up the topic with everyone you know? Do you pray for justice? Do you send money immediately and encourage others to do the same? Do you join an action committee against this happening again? How do you feel about your reactions now?

- Are there other people in your life who you feel "are to blame" for contributing to your negative behavior by inciting you during crisis situations? How can you take more responsibility for stepping away from their need to judge these situations? Do you recognize that making someone else *part of the problem* does not free you from also being *part of the problem*? How can you become *part of the solution* even if you share your life with someone who continues to be *part of the problem*?

- *Who would you like to be* the next time one of these dramatic situations transpires? What systems can you put in place to remind you to respond differently next time? List the kind of intentions you wish to send to these situations to *be the change.*

Are you willing to look at some of the relationships of your life where you have chosen to stop authentically interacting with another and therefore stopped the flow of truth between both parties? Do you recognize that you also stopped the love? What balls have you left sitting in your court at this time in your life?

- Breathe and pick up the first ball and look at it closely.— Which relationship does this ball represent?
- What were you "protecting" this person from, or were you protecting yourself from something?
- What do you now see about the result of your lack of authenticity in this relationship—What was lost?
- How can you put this ball back into play—Who do you need to be now to get things moving?

Do this with every relationship in which you stopped communicating authentically.

CHAPTER NINE

The Courage to Embrace Something New

Finding Balance

It is possible for each of us to find that special formula that works for our lives. Finding balance is a choice, a choice to let go of the things that no longer serve us and to make the choices to sustain success, joy, and fulfillment in our careers, relationships and in all parts of our lives. If we are out of balance and remain on this same trajectory, we will inevitably crash. We will be forced to change by the loss of work, disease, divorce, or some other tragic event, and then think *poor me, look at what happened in my life.* Why not choose to begin a new way of living now? Many of us, when we see that the arc of our life is taking us down, feel helpless to extract ourselves because our ego will not permit us to make a different choice. We may feel we have earned our place at the top of our company and we will do anything to keep it. Our pride is at stake. Our identity may be so bound up in our success that the idea of abandoning it is like losing our life support system. We see only a fearsome void instead of the potential for new learning.

We may be in relationships where we are incapable of stopping our constant control, disrespect, blame and accusations that are destroying us and the people on whom we are projecting. All the while, we are so sure that it is the other person being disrespectful, incompetent, stupid, and disconnected and it is the other person who is inflicting on us these terrible things. We continue badgering him or her until there is no longer a relationship at all. And really, if we were able to stop at any time along the way, we might have saved ourselves from our unceremonious fall. Why are we so incapable of extracting ourselves before we hit rock bottom? Why do we not choose to recognize when our ego is in control—when the *inmates are running the asylum*? Maybe because we needed this moment, this powerful *defining moment*, this crash to earth and the subsequent shattering of everything to finally see ourselves clearly. Maybe we needed to free ourselves, to make space for something different and to make new and dramatically different choices. This parting of the veils, which allows us to see our role in our crash, becomes our greatest gift.

I have always been fascinated by *defining moments* in all their awkward guises, from the most innocent, seemingly-insignificant events to the most tragic losses. What they all have in common is that life is never again the same. Every event forever after is labeled as *before* or *after* that moment. Every past occasion is also re-categorized, remembered as occurring *before* the infamous *defining moment*.

My mother used to call these *defining moments*—*"the straw that broke the camel's back."* Something breaks inside of us when we crash, and if we choose to see it clearly, and see our role in creating this situation, we can put the pieces back together in a very different way . . . or recreate more of the same suffering. *Defining moments* offer us a huge opportunity to create something new, if we are willing to—and if we have the courage to—put our shame aside, embrace our vulnerability and make different choices.

Those of us who know our potential for being workaholics can learn to make different choices to keep our pursuit of excellence in balance with our inner well-being or we too may crash. We are whole beings and it is unwise and unhelpful to compartmentalize our needs by fulfilling some and ignoring others. This concept of wholeness has helped me grow personally, and contributed to my own leadership skills. I was always touched by the complexity of the members of my project teams and how their performances were directly related to how much joy and fulfillment they had in their lives. If something was out of balance, their work suffered and that meant the project suffered as well. Good leadership deeply comprehends and supports this issue of balance, understanding fully that the whole person must be functioning or else the results of the individual, and consequently of the team, will not be satisfactory.

When I chose to study for and become certified as an executive life coach to assist my leadership skills, I did not realize it would dramatically alter who I was being in the world as well. I went searching for a certification program that truly embraced this *whole person* concept. I was familiar with some coaching methods that focused on certain elements of the individual and coached what the individual was *doing* by setting goals to improve performance and productivity, and others where the coaching was mentoring and motivational. Something about these types of coaching models seemed superficial and lacking the holistic element— who the person was *being* in every moment of their lives. I was looking for the kind of transformational coaching that held a person accountable for his or her life and had the power to make a dramatic difference; the kind of coaching that was a conduit for radical and lasting change that would show up in every part of a person's life, from the boardroom to the bedroom. I was prepared to be fiercely courageous by holding up the mirror so that others might see their role in the events of their lives. I was also ready to be a catalyst for their transformation and growth, even if that meant that some may reject me out of their unwillingness to accept the reflection being offered. I knew I must be *"willing to lose someone for their sake."* When I came across the Co-Active Coaching model, something resonated. The extensive training and certification process was a pleasure to complete because it helped me further my own personal transformation. I had become deeply committed and prepared to be a mirror for others.

In 2005, after years of giving regular lectures at CIMBA, the Consortium of Universities for International Studies here in my small town, I began to teach Leadership Behavior to MBA students, the Executive Program students and the affiliated undergraduate exchange students by using many of the principles discussed in this book. I was thrilled to see how much MBA programs had changed from the *rip-em, tear-em, kill-em dead* mentality of the 1980s and how powerfully CIMBA had embraced this new model of leadership and neuroscience. Their motto is to develop the leader within each individual through one-on-one coaching and to teach students by example to *persuade, motivate, inspire* and *assist* others to higher levels of performance. I loved my year at CIMBA and truly enjoyed using this forum to demonstrate *how our choices create our lives* within the framework of coaching students and helping them better understand leadership behavior. Over the years, I have assisted at CIMBA in any way I can, and as I complete the writing of this book, I am lecturing and coaching MBA students.

I have had the privilege of coaching many amazing individuals. I feel honored and grateful to bear witness to their daily moments of clarity and transformation, and the realization of their deepest desires and fulfillment of their dreams. Some people choose coaching because of difficult personal issues and some people come because of business challenges. The common denominator for all is a profound desire to create change in their lives and to achieve their greatest potential. When we passionately coach others with enthusiasm, inspiration, wisdom, honesty, fierce courage and joy, we affect their lives. They will go out into the world and *pay it forward* by influencing other people's lives. We set energy in motion and we exemplify what it means to *be the change.*

Choice → Change → Create

If we have the courage to believe that we can make a difference almost *instantly* by whoever we are being in the present moment, then we will choose to step up and make that impactful difference. If we sincerely comprehend that our deepest feelings of self-worth and value create our illusion, our *show,* and attract to us every relationship and circumstance of our lives, then we can decide now to write a different script. We get to focus on the positive, to stimulate our dreams, and to honor our values. If we understand the *Law of Attraction*, then we recognize we must consciously focus on what makes us feel good about our lives in order to attract into our lives all that we desire. We get to decide ahead of time to be happy—to let go of our stories, and to find the gift even in the darkest experiences. We have a choice in every moment of our lives what to think about and how to feel. If we have the courage to see that we have a role in everything, then we have the potential to take back our power. This is where we begin to make the **choice** that leads to **change** and will ultimately **create** something different.

Only we can dare to see every person and situation that crosses our path as a remarkable opportunity to honestly understand who we are being in every moment. When we resolve to be responsible for our every reaction to every situation, from our most intimate relationships to the global tragedies that impact us all, we will be exercising true leadership and moving toward consciousness. We will have learned how to make the kind of choices that contribute to being part of the overall solution.

Be disciplined, bold and visionary. Send love to every situation that confounds you. Send love to people you want to judge. Send love to the injustices you feel compelled to fight against. Send love when you are in doubt and when you are sure you are "right." Send love to all the dramas and stories you needed to create in the past and feel appreciation. Everything has happened perfectly the way it needed to in order to deliver you to this moment. Send love, compassion and then, hold steady, and let go.

Be authentic and walk your talk, knowing that people are desperately searching for role models. Find the best in everyone and be quick to demonstrate your love, patience, compassion and forgiveness. Everyone desires to be loved; when in doubt send people unconditional love and you will always be pleasantly surprised. Be respectful and kind to everyone that crosses your path. Listen in a way that honors another and in that way you will be teaching others how to listen too. Have the courage to see your role in everything and to make the kind of choices that will bring you into harmony with your dreams. Be 100% present in each moment and savor it. Remember that *life is not a dress rehearsal*—if you are not happy doing what you are doing, make a different choice. Be an example for others so that they may choose to learn how easy it is to be positive, to be enthusiastic and to live with passion and in joy.

If you are an example of all of these things, you will undoubtedly leave a profound impression. If you touch the lives of just five people who see how powerful you are, you will have taught them the same. They will touch the lives of five more people, who will touch the lives of five more people . . . and you will truly *be the change* while creating a critical mass of change . . . Why? . . . Because we are all connected . . . and we are all one.

Acknowledgments

This book is filled with the knowledge of many great individuals whose special gifts have been instrumental in enlightening my journey. The thousands of books and hundreds of lectures/ seminars on leadership, business, neuroscience, psychology, health, self-help, coaching and spirituality are too many to list . . . and a few must be celebrated.

To Deepak Chopra, who more than anyone changed my vision of the world, the presence of your words and wisdom has left an indelible mark on my life. Thank you for opening the door to your world and inviting me in.

To Arielle Ford who generously connects me to the world. She taught me about taking an active role in creating *Big Love,* and how to recognize it when it arrives. Thank you for nudging and inspiring me through the writing of this book with humor and wisdom. I have unlimited gratitude for the gift of your and Brian Hilliard's friendship and love in my life.

To Kersti Gløersen and Lennart Lööv whose unique journey, intense insight and deep friendship has informed and guided me more than any words can articulate. From you I have truly understood that I have all the wisdom within me, how to find that wisdom even in the darkest moments, and how to live in the present moment more fully and more often without feeling expectation or loss. It has been an honor and a pleasure to open our home so that you may present your transformational seminars in Italy.

To Wayne Dyer, Debbie Ford, Esther and Jerry Hicks, Eckhart Tolle, Neale Donald Walsch, Marianne Williamson and Doc Childre and the wonderful people at the Institute of HeartMath. Thank you for your brilliance and for your ability to present complex concepts in a way that shook my life . . . I am forever changed because of you.

To the fantastic Co-Active Coaching model and the certification process through The Coaches Training Institute (CTI), especially to my courageous coach Andy Denne and to my coaching companion and very dear friend Margo McClimans, and my fierce pod companions Frode Svensen and Carissa Bub. Your compassion and support along this journey was priceless.

For your generosity in offering to read this text and share your comments and wisdom—Thank you for your loving touch—Arielle Ford, Kersti Gløersen and Lennart Lööv, Margo McClimans, Laura Massarotto, Martha Pien, Dominic Standish, and Steve Green.

To my editor Danielle Dorman and my proof reader Sharon Berman for being able to leap in and make sense of everything— thank you for being exactly who and what I needed you to be.

I possess an indescribable gratitude for the friends and clients whose stories have made this book come alive. Their personal challenges and triumphs will live on by teaching others to make different choices. Thank you for sharing a piece of your life with me.

To my mentors Bob Babcock, Richard Griffiths and Al Ringleb, whose exacting standards stretched me at times when I thought there was nothing left to give. Thank you for helping me to see myself clearly.

To my friends who are the pillars of my life—you have been at my side for as long as I can remember—holding the mirror with steady and compassionate hands. Deep gratitude to Donna Paitchel, Arlene Avidan, Sara Galbraith, Robert Turner, Sara Fox, Despina Katsikakis and Stephen Blundell, Laura Massarotto and Martyn Walker, Sara and Tom Matthews, Max Steinkopf, Marcia Morris, Ronne Hackett, and Ellen Smoller.

I am so fortunate to have an amazing group of friends from around the world who contributed in numerous ways to the wisdom in this book and the richness of my life—Katiuscia Baggio, Kim Cameron, Christopher Cox, Kay Curtis, Licia Cusinati, Rosalyn Dexter, Joanita and Steve Green, Darlene Hart, Bing Howell, Cristina Modolo, Martha Pien, Cristina Romanello and Giovanni Casellato, Paula Silver, Antonis Stratoudakis, and Sheree Whatley . . . your presence in my life is a gift.

To my treasured siblings Leah Gallivan, Jim Picardi and Paula Reenstierna and their families who have listened to me talk about these concepts for years . . . thank you for your amazing humor, unlimited patience, boundless love and constant support.

To the amazingly special children of my husband – Alessandra Chiavelli and Guido Chiavelli – and to my wonderful extended Italian family and friends—Thank you for loving me and welcoming me with open arms into your homes and your lives.

ABOUT THE AUTHOR

Carla L Picardi – author, consultant, lecturer, TEDx and keynote speaker - has a degree in Architecture and Design, and over 40 years of experience in leading people to create a vision, and to make that vision a reality in design, property development, concept development, project management and people development. Carla was awarded the prestigious *Loeb Fellowship* at Harvard University - Graduate School of Design for her work on Canary Wharf, London UK, where she was one of the original eight people who created its concept, and one of the Project Executives who implemented Phase 1. Carla was the Project Director for the iconic Gherkin in London, which received the first planning permission in over 30 years for a tall building in the City of London and won the 2004 Stirling Prize for architecture.

Carla has been a Vice President for Citibank and Strategic Development Adviser to the BBC. She consults on architectural projects of all sizes, lectures on design, complex development projects, transformational leadership, coaching and various other topics. Carla was the Director of the Leadership Development Program at CIMBA where she helped create and implement a behavioral-based Leadership and Coaching program for the

International MBA, Executive and Undergraduate Exchange Programs. Carla wrote this book as an easy way to introduce these profound leadership principles to people of all ages. She is a Certified Professional CoActive Coach (CPCC) and coaches and mentors students and executives worldwide.

She lives in Asolo, Italy with her husband Goffredo Chiavelli.

Visit the author online at www.carlapicardi.com and explore Carla's TEDx at: https://www.youtube.com/watch?v=-Kd09B-1loQ

My Book List

These are some of the wise individuals who have profoundly touched my life and contributed to my worldview. Please enjoy every word of their wisdom ... and do not make these very human people gods or take their words as the truth for your life. Always use discernment and observe what feels good for you. Never confuse the man (or woman) with the message and/or *don't throw the baby out with the bath water.*

Deepak Chopra
Wayne W. Dyer
Arielle Ford
Debbie Ford
Doc Childre—HeartMath Team
Kersti Gløersen and Lennart Lööv
Esther and Jerry Hicks
Eckhart Tolle
Neale Donald Walsch
Marianne Williamson
Laura Whitworth, Henry Kimsey-House, Phil Sandahl (as well as their whole *Co-Active Coaching Certification*)

Other great authors who merit exploration:

Gregg Braden
Brené Brown
Jack Canfield

Doloros Cannon
Julia Cameron
Sonia Choquette
Stephen Covey
Joe Dispenza
Malcolm Gladwell
John M. Gottman
Daniel Goleman
John Gray
Gay Hendricks
Ihaleakala Hew Len
Wim Hof
Bruce H. Lipton
Lynne McTaggart
Dan Millman
Caroline Myss
James Nestor
Christiane Northrup
James Redfield
Gary Renard
Marci Shimoff
Daniel J. Siegel
Joe Vitale
Brian Weiss
Ken Wilbur

Best Practices of Meditation and Mindfulness:

Deepak Chopra — Meditation Techniques
Joe Dispenza — Unlimited Meditations
Wayne W. Dyer — Meditations for Manifesting
HeartMath — Freeze-Frame, Quick Coherence, Inner Balance
Esther and Jerry Hicks — Getting into the Vortex
Jon Kabat-Zinn — Mindfulness Based Stress Reduction
Loving Kindness Meditation